ASCENT TO HARMONY

לקראת התפארת

ASCENT TO HARMONY

by

Rabbi Elie Munk

זצ"ל

FELDHEIM

1987

First published 1987
ISBN 0-87306-407-0

Copyright © 1987 by
the Estate of Rabbi Elie Munk

All rights reserved

No part of this publication may be translated,
reproduced, stored in a retrieval system or transmitted,
in any form or by any means,
electronic, mechanical, photocopying, recording or otherwise,
without prior permission in writing from the publishers.

Philipp Feldheim Inc.
200 Airport Executive Park
Spring Valley, New York 10977

Feldheim Publishers Ltd.
POB 6525 / Jerusalem, Israel

Printed in Israel

CONTENTS

Introduction vii

PART I: From Genesis to Sinai
  1. In the Beginning Was Love 3
  2. In the Beginning Was the Ideal 4
  3. Man Is A Microcosm 5
  4. The Ten Fundamental Elements 6
  5. The Creative Role of Man 9
  6. The Four Worlds 11
  7. The Breath of Life—Movement and Change 13
  8. The First Sin and the Disruption of Harmony 15
  9. The Origin of Evil 18
10. Psychology of the Soul 20

PART II: Sinai—The Law of Harmony
  1. At Sinai: The Crossroads of History 27
  2. Seven Stages In the Creation of Israel 27
  3. Mysteries of G-d's Name 29
  4. Man's Dual Road to G-d Through Torah 34
  5. The Individual and Society 35
  6. Divine Guidance of Human Destiny 37
  7. Prophecy 38
  8. Struggle to Excel 40
  9. Tikkun—Restoration 42
10. The World's Spiritual Origin 44
11. The Meaning Behind the Mitzvos 45
12. The Relations Between Israel and the Other Nations ... 53
13. Holiness 56

PART III: To Redemption
1. The Harmony of Flesh and Spirit 61
2. The Harmony of Justice and Love 67
3. The Harmony of Reason and Faith 74
4. The Special Role of Love In Achieving Harmony 79
5. The Stages of Human History and the Kingdom of G-d . 80
6. Harmony Between Israel and Its Land 84
7. Ultimate Harmony 86

Biography 91

INTRODUCTION

The great ideal that gives beauty and meaning to creation is not perfection, but harmony. Perfection is a lofty and noble ideal, but it is fixed and static. Once perfection is reached progress must stop because there is nowhere to go. Perfection is a golden dead end; it leaves no room for further improvement. Harmony on the other hand is a dynamic, ongoing process. This is symbolic of life. It is the very *purpose* of life, for it is man's mission to harmonize the threads of his being, his talents, his thoughts, his actions, and his emotions so that he will be in harmony with G-d's creation.

The Zohar explains this principle in the lives of the patriarchs: Avrohom, Yitzchok, and Yaakov. Avrohom's life is symbolized by חסד, *lovingkindness* (or love). Yitzchok's life is symbolized by דין, *justice* (or law). These are two extremes, for feelings of love and kindness tend to push out beyond the limitations of justice, whereas the dictates of the law seem to demand punishment and deny kindness that has not been properly earned. And yet both love and justice are valid and necessary. What is needed is to find a proper blend—the harmony—of how much love and justice are necessary to achieve the ideal condition. This principle of harmony—known in Kabbalistic literature as תפארת, *splendor*, is symbolized by the life of Yaakov.

It is because of his role of harmony that Yaakov is described as the finest of the patriarchs; indeed, he is the one who dominates the structure of Jewish history as the בריח התיכון, *the central shaft*, which supported the structure of the tabernacle. Both Avrohom and Yitzchok produced offspring (Yishmoel and Esov) who were opposed to the goals of the developing Jewish nation; Yaakov alone was found worthy to have a family totally in harmony with these goals. It was his family that was chosen to give its name to the nation, בני ישראל; the *Children of Israel*.

This book, *Ascent to Harmony*, traces man's climb to this primary goal of his existence. Its arguments are drawn from and soundly based upon Kabbalistic teachings. These teachings become the foundation for an intellectual and emotional understanding of creation and history.

And what is Kabbbalah? It is a deeper discipline that combines rational ideas with those that are beyond man's full understanding. In this sense, Kabbalah and man are mirror images of one another. man combines mind and heart, intellect and emotion. The Kabbalah, too, combines our rational understanding of truth with higher truths that have both been passed down to us from teacher to student, beginning with the first Divine teachings that were given to man by the Almighty. ("Kabbalah" means to receive.)

These two, the intellect and the emotions, are the essential tools of Jewish philosophy, and they will appear constantly in our study. The *Rama* writes that Jewish rational philosophy and Kabbalah have a common meeting point, for there are striking similarities between Maimonides' philosophical writings and the esoteric Kabbalistic principles of *Tikkunei Zohar*. This commonality has been our guide throughout this work.

After much soul searching if this study is suitable for modern times, I undertook this project even though it appears to clash strongly with the mood of our scientific age. Today's world is fascinated by the worship of rational thought, the logical basis of our understanding of the physical world; metaphysics and mysticism are held in low esteem. This worldly atmosphere has even infiltrated the Torah world, by overstressing the study of the concrete and more easily understandable (נגלה) at the expense of the higher concepts of abstract thought (נסתר).

It is appropriate to refer to the famous Kabbalistic giant, the *Ari ZaL*, who admonished those who have the intellect to go beyond the literal meaning of the Torah (פשט) but who do not make the effort to reach beyond this basic level of Torah knowledge. The *Ari ZaL* felt that by this neglect we diminish the most important of all Mitzvoth, the study of Torah (ותלמוד תורה כנגד כולם) and so are guilty of not learning fully the Torah (ביטול תורה).

How exciting is the description of our Sages, who called Kabbalah, "the science of truth" (חכמת האמת).

There are those who are concerned by restrictions in the Talmud limiting the study of the secrets of the Torah (רזי תורה) to a few highly capable students. However, we must refer to the master בעל טל אורות who among many sages maintained that these restrictions do not apply to the sixth millenium in which we live. On the contrary, they stressed the importance of disseminating Kabbalah, basing themselves on the explicit admonition of the Zohar that the study and knowledge of the hidden wisdom (סתרי תורה) are essential to the final redemption of the world (הקדמה לרקאנטי).

I wish to extend my warmest and deepest feelings of gratitude for this English translation to Mr. E. S. Maser whose total devotion to this work and to the larger work, "Call of the Torah," is a perfect example of Torah dedication (תורה לשמה). Likewise to Mr. Yitzchok Kirzner for his skillful editing and his earnest efforts for an articulate and inspiring presentation.

It is my fervent hope that through this "Ascent to Harmony," we can become better able to attain the lofty goal of serving G-d.

משמיה דרבי עקיבה "והתפארת" זו מתן תורה (ברכות נ"ח, א')

Elie Munk
Brooklyn, N.Y.
חנוכה תשל"ח

PART I
FROM GENESIS TO SINAI

1. IN THE BEGINNING WAS LOVE

"עולם חסד יבנה"
(תהלים פ״ט, ג׳)

THE WORLD WAS BUILT WITH LOVE

The beginning of life is marked by the presence of a mysterious and invisible force: this force which we call love. ״כי האהבה הוא חסד) בכל מקום״ לבוש בספר טעמי המצות, מצוה ה).

Of all the mighty forces which make up this world, love alone has the power to develop a seed into a living being. Just as the sun rises over the endless sky, so does love rise above the restrictions of this earth. With supernatural creative power it presents to man the miracle of miracles, the miracle of birth.

Love is the first gift that G-d gave to mankind. This purest and most wonderful gift is independent of life and even of death. Who can doubt that love has come to us from some heavenly place, far beyond our lowly world?

Just as each day love watches over the cradle of human life, it long ago watched over the birth of life in the universe. For it was out of love that G-d created the heavens and the earth (דרך ה׳, חלק א פרק ב). The Almighty King existed before there ever was any kind of "existence" that we can understand. His Being has no need of such "existence." In fact, all that ever existed and ever can exist is part of G-d. Therefore, to visualize man's creation we must imagine G-d setting aside part of His Divine Being to the world of man.

So it is that G-d began His relationship with our universe out of love, a sharing of the Divine Self. Through an act of cosmic generosity G-d formed man in His image and gave to this creation the supreme gift of the Divine Being. In the act of creation G-d appeared to rearrange His all encompassing presence. This created the effect of a Divine withdrawal which made room for the existence of mankind. That act of self-sacrifice produced space.

However, the Absolute G-d did not diminish Himself by the act of creating the universe. Although He shared Himself with it and put His soul into it, He did not dilute His Divine essence. Without ever actually blending with this world, His essence continues to hover majestically over creation (עץ חיים, ענף א').

2. IN THE BEGINNING WAS THE IDEAL

Nature everywhere offers us spectacles of magnificent beauty but it is in man himself that we find the best insight into the Divine Majesty. There is in man a perfect harmony of spirit and matter, heaven and earth. Alone of all creatures, man has the freedom to throw off the chains of matter and climb up to reach breathtaking heights of the spirit.

The first man, created by G-d's own hand and in the fullness of His love, was a model of perfection. He was given mental powers and physical strength far greater than the weakened man of today can imagine. Even the power of creation itself was given to him.

Originally, Adam's destiny was to live a life full of Divine joy, delighting in the beauty of nature and in a close relationship with G-d. For that purpose, G-d put him in the garden of paradise with the condition that he tend the garden and preserve it.

In that ideal state, Adam did not know what sin was. He was not affected by the temptation to do bad. Evil simply held no attraction for him. As long as he did not taste the "tree of the knowledge of good and evil," his soul was bathed in purity and peace. It was filled with the infinite love of its Creator (דרך ה' פרק ג').

Every soul still secretly wishes for that wonderful joy. Every soul still feels nostalgia for its origins. In truth, it is possible, that at a high point in a person's life, he may have the good fortune of feeling a thrill of spiritual happiness as his entire being is suddenly carried to a height far beyond the temptations of this world. He then feels a dramatic increase in strength; he feels that he himself can create works that will last forever. In that state he comes in contact with the Infinite once again.

3. MAN IS A MICROCOSM

The early splendor of the soul in this world did not last long. Eating the forbidden fruit may seem to us like a small sin. Yet it was obviously very significant for it made Adam lose his paradise on earth. Not only that, the whole of nature went to its downfall along with man. Because of Adam's sin, nature became harsh and demanding. Man now had to sweat to get the food that he needed to live. His peaceful coexistence with the animal kingdom disappeared. The close harmony of creation changed into a struggle for existence.

Right from the start, we see that man's history is tied in with his relation to nature. The great happiness that the Creator had planned for man was linked to the harmony between man and nature. However, that harmony depended on man's moral value.

The world that G-d created consists of a balance of many forces. Some of these are physical, others are emotional, and others are spiritual. Although the existence of these forces is an unchanging fact, the way that they interact with each other depends on man. This is because man is created with two special qualities: he is the only creature who is composed of all the forces that make up this world and he has the power of free will. It is because of these qualities that man is given the responsibility for keeping nature in its perpetual state of balance.

The mineral, vegetable, animal, and spiritual worlds each contain a certain portion of this world's forces. Man is the only creature who shares in all. He is the meeting point of the universe. It is as though he were placed at the center of creation. In this sensitive position, he has his finger on the controls for all of nature. He is, in effect, the "ruler over nature" (עקידת יצחק שער י״ב).

Although man and nature depend on each other and are always

interacting, it is man who is in charge. Because of the power of free will, which man alone has, he can preserve or disturb the balance of nature. If man weakens the positive spiritual forces in the harmony of nature, he can tip the balance and unleash other forces, possibly highly destructive ones. The sensitivity of the universe is like that of the human body where a minor upset can lead to a severe illness.

G-d created this world in a state of equilibrium. Man stands upright in the middle of creation, holding sensitive balance scales. The slightest deviation or even a minor vibration could start oscillations which, if not stopped, might result in massive destruction. The harmony of the world is as if suspended on the point of a needle.

4. THE TEN FUNDAMENTAL ELEMENTS

Within this universe, there are countless worlds of reality, some of which are within our own experience, and some of which we can hardly imagine. Just consider how important to us is the world of the human body, the world of political groups, and the world of social classes. Each of these worlds is a complex structure, in itself a complete system for which there is an ideal state of equilibrium—a state of peace and harmony.

Each system or world of harmony is based on the universal harmony on which all of creation is founded (פרדס משער א׳ עד ח׳). That carefully balanced universal harmony is the source of true happiness and beauty. The universe is like a complex mechanism consisting of many delicately tuned components (wheels within wheels). When each component is balanced within itself and with the related parts, the whole reaches the state of harmony.

To understand this concept more fully, we need a valid model through which we can visualize the plan of creation.

Such a model is the concept of the ten fundamental elements of creation, the ten spheres. (We are using the English word "sphere" in a special sense here, chosen because of its similiarty to the Hebrew "ספירות" rather than because of its common meaning of a rounded shape. For our purposes it is best to think in terms of the phrase "sphere of influence," in which the word "sphere" describes a

To bring about this harmony, man must develop a true knowedge of the universe and of life. Far from being a superficial concept, harmony is the real result of an arduous search for balance among the powerful forces of the universe. When the forces of the universe are in balance, they unite in their common goal. Instead of destroying each other, the opposing forces of good and evil, spiritual and material, take their place in the universal orchestra of creation.

When this perfection is reached, human life becomes transformed. All of life becomes a deeply felt symphony in which each human soul vibrates in unison with the universal soul of creation.

Only man is capable of bringing this harmony of existence to the world. Man alone is responsible for returning the universe to its pre-established harmony.

6. THE FOUR WORLDS

As we discussed in Section 4, one way of visualizing the plan of creation is the model of the 10 spheres. However, the Kabbalists did not stop here. They gave us further insight into the connection between G-d and the world he created, using the concept of the four worlds (פרדס שער ט״ז). The four worlds are like the rungs of a ladder which man must ascend to find G-d. They are as follows:

(1) עולם האצילות—The abstract world of the ideal. It was in this world that the ideal of a perfectly balanced mankind was placed, long before creation. This world is now the region in which the L-rd determines each man's reward and punishment. Another name for this world is עולם המתקלא, the world of balance.

(2) עולם הבריאה—The world of creation; the world of underlying active forces.

(3) עולם היצירה—The world of formation. This is the world in which were formed intermediaries between heaven and earth, such as angels and natural laws (קל״ח פתחי חכמה כלל ל״ח).

(4) עולם העשיה—The world of action. This is the world of the senses and of experience.

How does this concept of the four worlds relate to our life? We can see it in a dream, the dream of our forefather Jacob. In Jacob's dream, he saw a ladder which was set on the earth, but which reached up to heaven. The Midrash tells us that the ladder had four rungs. It is these four rungs that symbolize how man must raise himself step-by-step through the four worlds to meet the presence of G-d.

The quest for truth must start from our own experiences in the world of the senses. From these experiences the mind extracts the natural laws or "forms" which guide the objects that we sense and which make them behave as they do. Then, by logical analysis the mind proceeds further, seeking the causes, the forces that create these forms. Finally, the mind penetrates to the Supreme Reason, which is the innermost soul and first cause of all else.

Our Sages handed down to us four methods of interpreting the Torah and its mitzvot (see part II chapt. 11). Rabbi Yisroel Baal Shem Tov teaches that these too correspond to the four worlds:

פשט, the rational explanation corresponds to עולם העשיה
רמז, the explanation through allusions, to עולם היצירה
דרוש, the talmudic analysis, to עולם הבריאה
סוד, the secret explanation, to עולם האצילות.

The Kabbalists relate the four worlds directly to the 10 spheres, using the concept of the four domains in which the spheres are grouped. Thus, the world of אצילות corresponds to the domain of the spirit with its three spheres of Inspiration, Intelligence, and Reason. The world of בריאה corresponds to the ethical domain with its three spheres of Love, Justice, and Harmony. The world of יצירה corresponds to the physical domain with its three spheres of Energy, Form, and Organic Life. Finally, the world of עשיה corresponds to the domain of history, the sphere of the Kingship of G-d, מלכות.

[EDITOR'S NOTE. For an extended discussion on how this concept affects the form of our daily Morning Prayers, refer to the author's *The World of Prayer* (Introduction). Feldheim Publishers.]

7. THE BREATH OF LIFE— MOVEMENT AND CHANGE

One of the mysteries of our existence is the secret of life. All living creatures are composed of tiny objects called cells, within each of which is a living force. Where did this force come from? What changes a cell from an object to the dynamic element? The answer to these questions is the *breath of life* from the L-rd which transformed an unformed world עולם התהו into an active, dynamic world, a world of eternal motion.

The special quality of life is change. By imprinting the breath of life upon his universe, G-d showed that He wanted it to be constantly renewed and refreshed.

G-d used the process of change as part of the scheme of creation. The living universe began with the principle of Justice, דין, as the dominant force in the ethical domain. However, the first change was introduced with the substitution of the principle of merciful Love, חסד. "When G-d saw that the world could not endure under the yoke of Justice, He brought mercy to the fore and joined it to Justice." (רש"י בראשית א, א)

From this point on, the destiny of Universal History and that of each individual came to depend on the interaction between the two pillars of Love and Justice. G-d chose to limit the application of Heavenly Justice in many more ways than we can possibly understand. Some of the considerations that we know of are:

1. The patience (forebearance) of G-d
2. Man's repentance inducing G-d's forgiveness
3. The postponement of punishment until the world to come
4. The share of the society in a given sin
5. The merit earned by the good deeds of ancestors
6. The merit earned by the righteous of the generation

We cannot possibly guess at the full workings of this interaction between Love and Justice. Only the Creator can assess if an individual's merits or sins will sway the balance in his favor. However, we do know that between Love and Justice, the force of Love on the right side of the balance will prevail over the force of Justice on the left. In the structure of the Sefirot, the sphere of חסד appears on the right, immediately below the spiritual spheres. It is the stronger, just as right is stronger than left, positive stronger than negative, active stronger than passive, and masculine stronger than feminine.

Our Sages expressed these ideas in their interpretation of the word חסד in the presentation of the 13 Divine Qualities: "The school of Hillel teaches, 'And abundant in goodness, ורב חסד' means that He leans toward goodness and mercy, מטה כלפי חסד: when the individual's merits and sins are of equal weight, He tips the scales of judgement in favor of the merits" (ראש השנה י"ז, א).

* * *

G-d again showed His use of change in the process of creation when it came to the makeup of man himself. Of course, right from the start man was intended to have two kinds: male and female (רש"י בראשית א, כ"ז). This is because absolute Unity can exist only in G-d, never on earth. Mankind followed the universal pattern of creation in the use of masculine and feminine elements.

However, the male and female forms were originally bound up within one body, facing away from each other. In this respect man was similar to a plant form. Botanists tell us that it is common among plants to have both male and female elements growing from different parts of the same stalk. It was while in this primitive form that man received the Divine blessing "Be fruitful and multiply". However, the reproductive act was then merely an instinctive bodily function. It did not involve the emotional feeling of two individuals coming together of their own free will in an act of mutual love.

To achieve this important principle of love within the very act of procreation, G-d "made for him a help at his side עזר כנגדו," and thus created Eve as a separate being (רמב"ן בראשית ב, י"ח). We are told that at this time "heaven and earth united for the first time to produce rain" (זוהר א', ל"ה ע"א). The dewy mist rising from the earth corresponds to the loving desire of the female for the male. Then, having formed clouds in the sky, the same moisture returns to water the earth. In the same way, the male is enabled to return the gift of love and to complete the act of union with the female. Man and wife are truly united only when they are face to face and so come together in love for each other.

Thus, it was through mankind that the masculine-feminine pattern of creation reached its true fulfillment in love. Masculine and feminine tendencies attract and repel each other simultaneously, thereby keeping a delicately balanced state of equilibrium. This pattern exists as the secret of the creative process throughout the physical and spiritual worlds of creation. Everything gives of itself, surrenders itself, to multiply and serve anew. Life is renewed when each creature is able to receive and then offer its services in turn. It then reappears ennobled, productive, and blessed. G-d chose mankind to be the crown of His creation. Thus, mankind was given the opportunity to copy his Creator, repeating the process of creation—with love.

8. THE FIRST SIN AND THE DISRUPTION OF HARMONY

What was Adam's sin? True, the Torah spells it out for us. But it teaches us also that we must look for the טעם נסתר, the hidden reason which led Adam to do as he did. The Kabbalists answer that, in his thoughts, Adam degraded the Divine Majesty, separating his concept of G-d into two parts. He could not bring himself to unify his understanding of the Absolute G-d, who created the universe with his grasping of G-d the Universal Presence, who dwells in and directs His creation.

When man allows himself to experience the desire for the forbidden fruit, his soul falls victim to evil forces which quickly drive him downhill. Once the ideal balance of forces is disturbed, he becomes involved with harmful influences which fight over his soul. Ultimately, these influences lure him into chaos. However, man is not driven into eternal disgrace. On the contrary, every individual remains totally capable of raising himself, of using his will to return to the highest stage of purity. Nevertheless, the task has become more complicated. To restore a system to balance is much more difficult than to keep it in its original state of equilibrium.

Right from Genesis the Torah teaches us the fundamental principle of the oneness of creation; everything is interconnected. Because of this, the fall of Adam affected not only himself; it brought about the downfall of his descendants and indeed of all nature. Just as one man's sphere of activity is interconnected with the other spheres of nature, so is one generation interconnected with the other generations of mankind.

Because of man's key position within creation, each of his words, thoughts, and deeds can cause echoes reaching the most distant and heavenly spheres. Also, becasue of natural heredity, he can have a profound influence on his offspring, for good or evil. Thus, a man's action is like a stone dropped into a pond. It causes repercussions in breadth like the waves that travel outward to the distant edges of the pond, and it causes repercussions in depth as the stone descends downward through the layers of deep water.

The effect of the first sin on man's relationship to nature was tragic. However, the effect on the earthly presence of G-d, the Shekhina, was more tragic still. Before the sin the Divine Voice had spoken to Adam as one man speaks to another, telling him what was good and what was evil; as soon as Adam sinned, the Divine Presence fled from him. Adam had caused the first exile of the Shekhina (בראשית רבה י״ט, י״ג).

Originally a perfect unity and harmony existed between heaven and earth, between G-d and the world He created. Adam brought about a separation between them; he thereby destroyed the Divine order in the universe. The shock of this disruption unleashed a confusion between good and evil in all the spheres.

Although the "exile of the Shekhina" has been a curse for humanity, it has at times been a blessing for the people of Israel. Whenever Israel has gone into exile, the Shekhina has remained close by. "From this", teaches Rabbi Shimon Ben Yochai, "you realize how great is G-d's love for Israel" (מגילה ל״ג, א). By accompanying Israel into exile, the Shekhina has chosen to protect the people of Israel from the many dangers that lie in wait as Israel carries out its momentous task amid the nations of the world.

In commenting on Israel's experience in Egypt, Rabbi Chaim Ben Attar refers to Rabbi Shimon Ben Yochai's teaching to develop his view of the role of Israel in exile: "The mission of the chosen people is to reunite the sparks of light which lie smouldering under the ashes of a fallen humanity. By joining together the separate sparks of light, Israel will re-establish the Divine radiance that filled the world with holiness at the beginning of creation." (בראשית מ"ו, ג).

Rabbi Chaim Ben Attar continues: "Israel's mission as it wanders among the nations of the world is to reassemble all the elements of good which were scattered throughout mankind since the fall resulting from the first sin. To do this, Israel must free these elements from the thick shell (קליפה) covering them, and then recast and reconstitute them into a "great nation."

Since the universe was created as a balanced system, its positive forces are proportional to its negative forces. Thus, the more a particular place has the qualities of impurity (טומאה), the more it contains the potential of holiness (קדושה). It is for this reason that in early history the land of Egypt offered the greatest possibility for Israel to raise themselves to holiness. In Egypt the spirit of impurity from perversion and immorality had reached all "49 gates of impurity." Thus it was here, in the "iron furnace" of discipline and self-denial, that Israel could gradually rise up through the 49 gates of holiness. Only in Egypt could Israel really become a "great nation," the nation which G-d referred to as "גוי גדול," a great people.

After Adam's sin, the great task of restoration (Tikkun) began. This task of repairing the spiritual damage done to the universe became the responsibility of Adam's descendants. The kabbalists refer to it as the reunification of the two aspects of G-d that we have referred to: the Absolute G-d, who created the universe, and the Universal Presence (the Shekhina), who dwells in and directs His creation.

The unification of these two aspects of G-d is expressed in the prayer "לשם יחוד קב"ה ושכינתיה." It is also expressed as the joining of the first two letters of the Divine name ("Yod" and "He' ") with the last two letters ("Vav" and "He' "). The first two letters signify G-d the Creator; the last two letters signify the Shekhina.

9. THE ORIGIN OF EVIL

The story of creation declares that "G-d saw all that he had made and, behold it was very good." Why then does evil exist in the world? Furthermore, does it not say in the Psalms of David, "The L-rd is good and merciful over all His works" Why then did the prophet Isaiah proclaim, "He who forms the light and creates darkness, who makes peace and creates evil" (ישעיה מ״ה, ז)? True, those who composed our prayers softened these words when they made them part of our daily morning service. Instead of *Who creates evil*, the prayer reads *Who creates everything*. However, the meaning did not change, for the word *everything* includes evil.

To answer these questions, let us turn first to Maimonides' interpretation of the origin of evil (Guide for the Perplexed III, 8-12). Maimonides tells us that evil originates from G-d only in the sense that He is the Creator of matter, which is the basis for evil. Just as the essential quality of matter is its lack of form, so are evils essentially a withholding of G-d's presence, rather than some direct act of G-d. Man alone is the maker of evil, which results mainly from his ignorance—the veil of matter cuts off his knowledge of the Supreme Good, of G-d. Most evils affecting an individual or mankind as a whole are brought about by man's actions.

Furthermore, Maimonides reminds us, man is but an atom in the universe and is not the only product of creation. Although he sometimes appears to be struck by unexplainable evil happenings, this should not prevent him from sensing the ultimate good in creation. Everything necessarily originates from the Divine wisdom, but man is unable to understand the true purpose of everything that he sees happening in this world.

The Kabbalists also refer to evil as a shell (קליפה). Evil is like the shell or peel of a fruit, being necessary to the completeness of the fruit and yet being removed from the center. Its very existence requires that it be distant from the center. (פרדס שער היכלות הקליפות).

18

To better understand the purpose of evil in this world, we must investigate the question of justice and its relationship to evil. If creation was an expression of G-d's love, why did it have to include the harshness of justice? The answer lies in the essential quality of free will which characterizes man's existence in this world. With free will man can express his love for his Creator voluntarily, in a way that an angel could never hope for. However, free will implies the possibility of not choosing good and there must be a force within creation and within man to induce him not to do good. This essential force is present throughout creation. It is the force which we call evil (רע), even though it serves the good purpose of creation. Similarily, freedom of choice implies a system of reward and punishment; that is, of justice. Without justice there is no standard by which man's choice of good can be measured. If both the doers of good and the doers of evil were to be rewarded, the system of free will would be empty of meaning.

"גם את זה לעומת זה עשה אלקים," wrote King Solomon in Ecclesiastes (7:14). He created Hell as well as Paradise, unclean along with the clean, matter together with spirit. The elements of nature gravitate around the positive and the negative. It is therefore understandable that certain forces gain strength from the negative. Such forces include sorcery and witchcraft. Their power is real, but relative and limited. (פסחים ק״י, ב׳).

One should not be surprised to discover the presence of evil first mentioned in the creation chapter, and to see it presented as "very good." When viewed as part of the whole, evil makes a necessary contribution to the excellence of creation. The presence of different types of evil is as important to the harmony of creation as is the presence of base metals in contributing to the hardness of an alloy.

It is in this sense that Rabbi Meir said, "טוב מאד זה המות," very good includes even death." As long as the various types of evil are held under control, they serve the common good, just as do human passion and the elemental forces of nature.

In a brief summary, Rabbi S.R. Hirsch draws the following conclusion regarding the origin of evil: Although matter appears imperfect, G-d introduced it into creation as part of a Divine Plan. Because it is the plan of G-d, creation must be able to reach full perfection and must contain within itself all of the necessary elements to do so. It is up to man to determine what these elements are and to bring them into action in order to see the work of the six days of Creation brought to complete perfection.

When we speak of a covenant, we tend to think of a pact made between equal partners. Although man was created in the image of G-d, it is obvious that we cannot speak of an equality in referring to the covenant between G-d and man. However, if we look further it soon becomes apparent that equality is not necessary in a covenant. When nations make treaties they do not have to be equal to each other to form a covenant. All that is needed is a common ground in the identity of the parties involved. This common ground among nations, large and small, is an accepatnce by each other's sovereignty of the other's right to choose their own destiny.

If the relations between G-d and man were only those of Master and servant, the making of a covenant would clearly be deprived of this common ground. But G-d has granted man a privileged position in His creation sufficient to raise man to the level of a partner in a series of Divine covenants.

The first covenant was made between G-d and all of mankind. The Torah records it in the passage describing Noah and his sons leaving the ark. There we find the characteristics which are common to all covenants, a commitment or promise by each party and a symbol of the covenant. The commitment that G-d made on this occasion was never again to unleash such a cataclysm on the world. The commitment made by mankind was to build their lives on moral principles, contained in the seven laws for Noach's descendants. The symbol was the rainbow. The rainbow is a display produced as the direct result of a law imposed by G-d on nature to provide a symbol meaningful to mankind. "The Torah is expressed in the language of man." (ברכות ל״א, ב׳).

10. PSYCHOLOGY OF THE SOUL

The human soul is not bound by time or space. Just as G-d, the Universal Soul cannot be fixed in the finity of creation, so is the human soul not limited to a person's life span or a person's body (פרדס שער הנשמה).

When the soul enters the body, its state is described as pure

PART II
SINAI
THE LAW OF HARMONY

1. AT SINAI: THE CROSSROADS OF HISTORY

The history of the Jewish people illustrates a basic truth: man finds G-d by searching for Him with all the might of his soul. G-d answers man's search and helps him, but only after man has made the first effort.

So it was at Sinai: the continuing call rising from earth triggered an outpouring of Heavenly love. At that moment, when Israel was alone with G-d in the wilderness, G-d answered the love from below by revealing to Israel a knowledge of His most intimate Being. The Torah, which would change the world, was born.

At Sinai the paths of Israel and the other nations separated. (דרך ה׳ חלק ב, פרק ד). At that point of history, man was given a choice between two ways by which he could get knowledge of the Divine order for universal harmony. One way, chosen by the other nations, was the long and difficult road of experience. The other way, chosen by Israel, was through an act in which G-d revealed His plan directly. By this choice, Israel became forevermore the depository of the secret of universal harmony.

Sinai represents the cross-roads of history. Man, who is powerless to find salvation without G-d's help, was forced to choose one of two ways. Israel selected one and the nations the other.

2. SEVEN STAGES IN THE CREATION OF ISRAEL

Since the seven days of creation, the number seven has always had a special significance for measuring stages of development. For example, the seven weeks from Pesach to Shevuos represents the time needed to develop a people of slaves into a holy nation.

And so it was that the development of the nation of Israel from its first beginnings took place in seven distinct stages. In each stage Israel added new qualities to its character; with the end of the seventh stage, Israel reached its final form.

The first of the seven stages was initiated by Abraham. He marked this stage with the enthusiasm by which he expressed his love for G-d and man. This enthusiasm was the first characteristic of Israel.

The second stage has Isaac's imprint. To the burning love of his father, Isaac added a necessary balance: absolute obedience to the Divine commands. Isaac demonstrated this by having his body tied on the altar, ready to be sacrificed to G-d's will. That unwavering discipline became the second characteristic of Israel.

The third stage has the stamp of Jacob. In his personality he managed to combine love and obedience. He built on the heritage received from his father and grandfather to raise 12 sons. So it was that he established the Jewish ideal of family life based on tradition passed down from generation to generation.

The fourth stage is represented by Joseph. He personified Israel's ability to resist the seductions of immorality (Potiphar's wife) and political power (Pharaoh).

The fifth stage is the establishing of a national constitution by Moses the lawgiver.

The sixth stage is the introduction of the temple service by Aaron the High Priest. With this Divine service, Israel was brought to the stage of holiness.

The final stage in the formation of our people was the establishment of Israel's sovereignty as a nation in its land during the reign of King David.

The historic holidays of the Jewish year have given us a living and lasting expression of Israel's seven stages. By means of these holidays we are again and again reinvigorated in the exciting atmosphere of our origins. Each year as the nation passes through these stages as expressed in its holidays, it draws new moral and spiritual strength from the very roots of its creation.

The yearly cycle begins with the festival of Pesach, reminding us of the love between Israel and G-d that blossomed into Israel's existence as a nation. This was the love that we inherited from our father Abraham.

Shevuos marks the second stage. It commemorates the vow of everlasting allegiance through which the nation received the Torah at Sinai. This vow depended on the disciplined commitment which we inherited from our father Isaac.

The following stage is the festival of Succos in which we celebrate the quality that we inherited from our father Jacob. This festival reunites the whole family in the Succah which symbolizes the protection of the Almighty.

The festival of Succos has an extension which is considered an independent holiday. It is the closing festival (Shemini Atseres and Simchas Torah) devoted to the joy of the Torah. Through it we relive the historic phase characterized by the life of Moses, the teacher of the Torah to his people in the name of the L-rd.

The historical stage of Aaron who kindled the Menorah in the holy temple is expressed in Chanukah, the festival of light. Chanukah reminds us of the restoration of the holy temple in Jerusalem under the guidance of the priestly descendants of Aaron, the Chashmonoim (Hasmoneans).

The holiday of Purim reminds us of Israel's national resistance under Esther. This was inspired by the spirit of Joseph, the heroic defender of Judaism in pagan surroundings.

The seventh stage, that of King David, still awaits fulfillment. The "festival of David" will be celebrated only with the coming of the Messiah, the son of David, who will build the kingdom of G-d. "On that day I will raise up the fallen Tabernacle of David, I will repair its breaches, I will raise up its ruins, and I will rebuild it as in the days of old" (Amos 9:11).

3. MYSTERIES OF G-D'S NAME

Before we can study the mysteries of Creation we must realize that such knowledge is limited, not only by our human intelligence but by Divine decree.

In the Book of Proverbs (25:2), King Solomon said: "The glory of G-d is to conceal a thing; but the glory of the King is to search out a matter." This strange verse was explained by our Sages as follows: "The glory of G-d is to conceal a thing" refers to the first chapter of the Bible and requires us to respect the mystery of the work of creation (Maaseh Bereshit) and the related concept of the Throne of the Divine Majesty (Maaseh Merkava). However, starting from the second chapter of the Bible, "the glory of the King" yearns to be discovered through a clear analysis of the Biblical text (ילקוט שמעוני שם).

Accepting the limitations described above, the great Jewish Kabbalists worked to come closer to G-d through a study of His mysteries. Since the Torah, the work of G-d, was revealed to Moses in the form of a book composed of words and letters, the sages dug deeply into the analysis of those words and letters in order to discover Divine truths.

Among the best known Kabbalistic works is the "Book of Creation" (Sefer Hayetsirah), generally believed to be authored by Abraham who by means of letters and their numerical values revealed the fundamental principles of creation. The following discussion is therefore based on this concept. In it we investigate the letters that make up the name of G-d and the word "sefiros." To do this we must make a distinction between the alphabets of other languages and the Hebrew alphabet. Whereas other alphabets serve only as a means to form words in normal speech or writing, the Hebrew alphabet is the means which G-d chose to reveal His Divine powers.

The sages associate the letters in the Bible to the many "Divine Names," that is, to Divine powers. In this sense, we can view the Bible as sort of a code book containing the mysteries of Creation. However, the combinations of letters that form the words and phrases in the Bible have a literal meaning which we can understand. The essence of the Biblical alphabet is thus derived from a spiritual, Divine alphabet. In a similar manner, our concept of G-d is a spiritual, abstract one, and yet we can relate this to the concrete world in which He is revealed.

Even without knowing the Divine power associated with each letter and with each of the thousands of possible combinations of the 22 letters of the alphabet, it is possible to bring out certain ideas about the general principle. We start with the rule that each of the 22 letters relates to one fundamental Divine power. When combined, they symbolize the effect of the Divine powers in producing a certain condition.

For example, the Book of Creation defines the Name of G-d as being composed of 32 letters. These include the creative essence of each of the 22 letters of the alphabet and 10 letters that correspond to the 10 values of the Sefiros.

We have said that the 22 letters of the alphabet, taken individually, define the essence of the Divine powers. If we now take the 22 letters in combinations of two at a time rather than one at a time, we find that there are 231 possible combinations of letter pairs (Aleph-Beis, Aleph-Gimel, Aleph-Daled, etc.) This number 231 symbolizes the existence of Israel. In fact, the word ישראל is made up of יש-ראל, meaning it exists through 231 (the numerical value of ראל is 231).

To calculate the number 231, mathematicians use a standard formula for the number of combinations possible in a series of things taken two at a time. This formula is $n(n-1)/2$. For example, for the four letters A, B, C, D there are six combinations of letter pairs (AB, AC, AD, BC, BD, CD). To calculate this number from the formula, simply substitute 4 for n. This results in $4(4-1)/2$ or 6. Similarly the number of pairs in a series of 22 things is calculated as $22(22-1)/2$ which comes out to 231.

The Kabbalists say that Israel's existence derives from the 231 Gates of Heaven. This idea underlines the importance of the letters of the Biblical alphabet and their many mathematical combinations.

We have described the 10 Sefiros as a model for the creation of the world by G-d. They are also a model for man's participation in creation in partnership with G-d. Thus, we can uncover another level of meaning in the concept of Sefiros by examining the root of this word: ספר. The three letters of the root can make three words, which despite different meanings, support each other in forming a perfect unity.

1. ספר (counting) the expression of intelligence
2. ספר (telling) the expression of speech
3. ספר (writing) the expression of action

These three functions are the essential parts of the creative power as visualized and experienced by man.

The 10 Sefiros are not only part of the 32-letter name of G-d;

they are also connected with His name of 4 letters, which is introduced in the second chapter of the Bible and is often referred to by the Greek word Tetragrammaton.

The first letter of the Tetragrammaton is *Yud*, the smallest letter of the alphabet. It resembles the initial seed of purest spirit from which the 10 Sefiros grew.

The first two letters of the Tetragrammaton *Yud* and *Hei* form the 2-letter name of G-d, symbolizing G-d the original Creator. For example, our Sages interpreted the words of the prophet Isaiah (26:4) "Trust in the L-rd forever, for with *Yud* and *Hei* did G-d create worlds," that is, G-d created the upper world with the letter *Yud* and G-d created the lower world with the letter *Hei*. The upper world refers to the domain of the first three Sefiros, also called the spiritual domain (אצילות). The lower world refers to the three Sefiros of the ethical domain (בריאה).

The letter *Yud* is thus the male factor, the dynamic source of energy. It finds its partner in the letter *Hei*, passive and receptive in nature. The letter *Hei* therefore becomes the mark of this world, which borrows its vital force from the spiritual world.

The second half of the Tetragrammaton *Vav* and *Hei* reveals G-d as the invisible One Who continuously sustains and guides the existence that He created (Shechinah). The world of formation (יצירה), that is, the physical domain with its spheres of energy, form, and organic life is symbolized by the letter *Vav*. Just as the physical domain is a link between the world of angels and our world, so is the letter *Vav* a linking symbol. When used as a prefix it represents the word "and," joining the next word to the one going before. Its numerical value is six, corresponding to the six days of creation in which the link was forged. Because it is a link, the number six falls at the center of the range of the ten numbers which identify the ten spheres.

As for the letter *Hei*, the last letter of the Tetragrammaton, it identifies the fourth world (עולם העשיה), the world of action. Although called the world of action, it is seen as passive in the sense that it depends on the unfolding of history, the actions of mankind. These will ultimately achieve the completion of this world by the universal acknowledgement of the Name of G-d. "In that day the L-rd will be One and His Name One."

The universal recognition that G-d alone is the source of all existence and all creatures is symbolized by the compactness which characterizes the letters of the Tetragrammaton. The three letters used in this word, when spelled out, have the smallest numerical values of any letters in the alphabet (י״ד = 14, ה״י = 15, and וו = 12). That smallness corresponds to the idea of the productive seed, as mentioned earlier with respect to the letter *Yud*.

The Tetragrammaton also carries within itself a picture of how G-d's name is revealed to this world over time: past, present, and future, according to the four stages of the 10 Sefirot. Thus, the origin of creation is in the first sphere (כתר) of the spiritual world, expressed in the letter *Yud*. The next two letters *Hei* and *Vav* bring us from the past to the present by means of the ethical and physical worlds, which are the foundation for the continuing process of revelation. Finally, the letter *Hei* symbolizes the future, the world of Kingship (מלכות), which is the basis for the coming of Moshiach.

The idea of past, present, and future in the development of G-d's revelation is also expressed in our daily prayers ברכות קריאת שמע. The first of the three Brochos of the Shema pays tribute to the origin of creation (יוצר המאורות); the second (הבוחר בעמו ישראל באהבה) praises the continuing experience of Divine revelation; and the third (גאל ישראל) speaks of our faith in the future, the redemption of Israel by Moshiach. These three Brochos, ending with the deliverance of Israel, symbolize the three pillars on which Judaism stands: Creation, Revelation, and Messianic Redemption (See the author's "*World of Prayer*" page 116).

We referred earlier to the fact that the first two letters of the Tetragrammaton symbolize G-d the Creator and Originator of our existence (Boreh) and the last two letters symbolize G-d the One who sustains and guides our existence (Shechinah). At the beginning of creation, the flow of blessing from the origin to the continuing life of the world was a smooth one. This is symbolized by the linking of the first two and the last two letters in one Holy Word. However, with man's sin, the flow of blessing had to be interrupted and the perfect union was disturbed. Man's sin had affected the form of G-d's presence in the world. By doing good deeds (Mitzvos) we work to heal this fault-line and return the form of G-d's name to the way it was. This is expressed in the words לשם יחוד קודשא בריך הוא ושכנתיה which the kabbalists introduced as a preface to be said before doing each Mitzvah—"for the sake of the union of the [the name of] the Holy One, blessed be He, with His [name of] Shechinah."

4. MAN'S DUAL ROAD TO G-D THROUGH TORAH

The Torah is the way that G-d has chosen to reveal Himself to man. The road is open. By following the Torah, man will ultimately find G-d.

There are two aspects to Torah, that which is seen—the visible letters—and that which is heard—the vowels and musical notations. (That which is heard, the sound of the Torah, can further be extended to include the תורה שבעל פה, the Oral Torah which Moses passed on to the generations of Israel by word of mouth.)

In the preceding chapter we discussed the discovery of G-d through the visible letters of the Torah and their numerical values. To do this, we made use of the analytical technique of the human mind which allows us to form a concept and to express it by a number. However, this technique is only one of the two pillars at the doorway of the mind. We may call it the left pillar, because it demands strict mathematical precision to make it correspond to the sphere of "Din," Justice.

Alongside the pillar of דין rises the pillar of חסד, of generous love. This leads to something quite different from the domain of visible letters and numbers. Instead we enter the domain of sounds, the world of music, the world of the mind's emotions. Through the exercise of our emotions we find a second way to G-d's sanctuary, a way which is equally valid.

When the Divine Spirit reveals itself, the letters of the alphabet give us the body, the anatomy of that which is revealed. The soul which makes the anatomy come alive is in the vowels and human pronunciation of the letters and words. If we now add the emotional expression of the טעמי המקרא (musical accents for Torah reading), the soul becomes free to soar to spiritual heights on the wings of sound.

The world of numbers and the world of sounds come from the same source and lead to the same objective. That is why they have certain characteristics in common. The world of numbers is based on mathematical relationships and patterns; the world of sounds is founded on patterns of rhythm and melody. But both tend to merge in the pure and holy heights of the world of the spirit (אצילות) and both extend their roots into the nutritive soil of the world of creation (בריאה).

Because the human mind is built to function in both the world of numbers and the world of sounds, man should use both abilities in climbing the spiritual ladder. Why choose between the right hand and the left hand? You will be much more likely to arrive at your destination if you choose both. As you begin discovering the riches in words, letters, and vowels you will find a new light illuminating each step of your climb. That which seemed difficult and contradictory at a lower level seems to resolve itself as you rise along your spiritual path. You are on the royal road to the knowledge of G-d.

5. THE INDIVIDUAL AND SOCIETY

Maimonides begins his ideas about society with the following comments on human nature (Guide for the Perplexed Part II Chap. 40): Man is naturally a social being and his nature demands that he live in society. Because of the great variety of individual human beings, we can almost never find two people exactly alike in any moral quality or external appearance. Such a variety can be found in no animal species. The differences between individuals of every other species is limited; only man forms an exception.

When viewed as a book of laws, the Torah may be said to have two objectives: the well-being of the soul and the well-being of the body. For men to have well-being of the soul they need sound and wholesome ideas, each man according to his abilities. The Torah deals with this need sometimes explicitly, sometimes through allegory, for most men will not be able to understand a subject in its total reality.

For men to have well-being of the body, the law seeks to improve the conditions of life in society. This is accomplished in two ways: first, by preventing the exercise of violence of the stronger upon the weaker; second, by having each person acquire habits useful to social life so that the interests of society will be safeguarded.

The well-being of the body calls for physical health. This depends on the availability of the necessities of life—food, clothing, hygiene, shelter. In most cases, a man isolated and alone could never manage that, but society provides him with his needs.

In comparing the well-being of the soul with the well-being of the body, one must realize that the well-being of the soul is undoubtedly on a higher plane. Nevertheless the well-being of the body is the more urgent and must come first. Thus, the laws regarding the regulation of society are elaborated in minute and precise detail. Only after insuring the well-being of the body can man rise to the ultimate perfection, the well-being of the soul.

The well-being of the soul demands an "active intelligence," so that through the process of thinking and reflection man can reach all of the knowledge and understanding of which he is capable. Clearly this is not likely to happen when man is tormented by pain or physical discomfort.

This basic truth explains why the Torah was proclaimed more than 2000 years after Creation. Priority had to be given to the natural order.

Right from their beginning, the nations of the world received the seven commandments "of the children of Noah," the universal moral code for the human race. This code contains the "natural laws" and deals with the behavior and obligations of all human beings, not specifically Jews. Unhappily, the nations disregarded the universal laws, with the exception of those righteous individuals among them who are assured of their share in the world to come (דרך ה׳ חלק ב, פרק ד).

To achieve the proper balance between the individual and society is indeed the main problem of our times. Various totalitarian regimes have attempted to resolve it by freeing man's conscience from the obligations of religion and replacing it with the yoke of artificial economic or nationalistic structures. They have been unsuccessful because they have refused to accept the restrictions of a moral base for the actions of man and society.

And yet the prophet Micah declares to us that in the time of Moshiach, each nation will come to praise G-d with its own specific character: "For all the peoples will walk each one in the name of its god, but we will walk in the name of the L-rd. כי כל העמים ילכו בשם אלהיו (מיכה ד)." Unity will be formed from the individuality of the nations, oriented to a common ideal and based on Divine morality.

6. DIVINE GUIDANCE OF HUMAN DESTINY

The philosophers of many nations have agonized over the apparent conflict between the idea of free will and G-d's control over human destiny. Maimonides discusses the weaknesses in the solutions presented by the ancient philosophers and then goes on to present the only true view.

This is the view which guided the Jewish prophets and sages. The world is governed by natural laws, moral laws, and the Divine Hand (also referred to as Providence). The natural laws are the laws of physics and chemistry; they are like the laws which control the operation of a machine once it has been set in motion. Providence watches over the natural laws and intercedes as necessary to safeguard the well-being and continued existence of each basic type of creature: "השגחה כללית." The machine is never allowed to run away with itself. However, each individual animal does not receive the benefit of this special protection. The fate of the individual insect or fish is determined by the natural laws.

The moral laws are applicable only to mankind. They represent the standards by which each individual human being is expected to guide his actions. Those actions are free and will result in Divine reward or punishment in accordance with the moral laws. However, to the extent that the individual develops his moral sense and approaches moral perfection, he receives a corresponding degree of special Divine attention and protection: "השגחה פרטית." Thus, G-d watches with special care over those individuals who dedicate themselves wholeheartedly to His service. (Guide of the Perplexed part III chapt. 18)

The special feature of the Torah view is that it recognizes, that the differences between one man and the next can be substantial. The non-Jewish philosophers saw mankind only as a uniform mass and lost sight of man's individuality.

It is not known whether Maimonides knew kabbalah. An old

tradition has it that at the end of his life Maimonides expressed regret that he had not learned Kabbalah. In any case, we see that his understanding of this philosophical question is similar to that which the kabbalists would later teach in greater detail.

In his kabbalistic work entitled "Shiur Kumah," Rabbi Moshe Cordovero identifies ten cases in which G-d's special attention (Providence) plays a decisive role in human destiny. He also examines those cases in which this special attention vanishes completely, in accordance with the verse: "ואנכי הסתיר אסתיר פני ביום ההוא," and I will surely hide My face in that day" (Deut. 31:18). It is under such conditions that the innocent are carried away with the guilty as indicated in the Talmud: כיון שניתן רשות למשחית אינו מבחין בין צדיקים לרשעים, "Once permission is given to the angel of destruction, he does not distinguish between the righteous and the wrongdoers" (Bava Kama 60a). In another case of הסתר פנים, "the concealment of Providence," the Talmud speaks of a man who died innocently before the verdict of the heavenly tribunal was revealed (Chagiga 4b). The Talmud calls this a situation of יש נספה בלא משפט, "those who are swept away without judgement" (Proverbs 13:23).

The intervention of Providence on earth is governed by the two instruments of justice and love. Only G-d knows in what circumstances he uses one or the other, or when He allows natural laws to take over. However, we do know that the balancing of the two instruments of justice and love is done to further G-d's plan for the world. The tension between the two instruments determines the ongoing history of the universe as though the universe itself were on trial.

7. PROPHECY

What is prophecy? Is it some kind of sixth sense through which G-d makes His words known to the nation? Rabbi Judah Halevi in his Sefer Ha-Kuzari sees prophecy as more than that. He explains that the prophet undergoes a major transformation, becoming very different from what he was before (מאמר ד, ט״ז).

For Maimonides on the other hand, prophecy is the climax of an intellectual effort which leads gradually to the knowledge of G-d.

Man must undergo a long intellectual, moral, and physical training before arriving at its source (הלכות יסודי התורה פרק ז). Those who are in the midst of this training period are referred to as "בני הנביאים," the disciples of the prophets (I Kings 20:35).

Like Maimonides, the Kaballah distinguishes different stages of prophecy, extending to the topmost rung (שיעור קומה ט״ז). These stages are related to the ten sefirot, so that the topmost rung corresponds to the spiritual domain, "אצילות."

With respect to the inner character of Moses and Aaron, the kabbalists explain that the two sefirot of "נצח והוד," Energy and Form represent the roots of the two brothers' souls. Even though they are in the physical domain, "יצירה," these two sefirot symbolize the potential of man's subconscious, the voice of intuition.

When this potential is developed, the prophet reaches to "אצילות."

However, not all prophecy is at the same exalted level as that of Moses and Aaron. One of our sages teaches that when the Temple was destroyed, prophecy was withdrawn from the prophets and given to the weak-minded and children (בבא בתרא י״ב, ב). This reduced level of prophecy is referred to by the Talmud as "small prophecy." The power of "small prophecy" is derived from the same power that inspired the prophets. It is possible to ask a child, "Tell me what verse you have been learning?", and because of the power of small prophecy to trust in the child's reply.

How can we reconcile the idea of "small prophecy" with the intellectual demands of prophecy as taught by Maimonides? We can do this by following the kabbalists teaching of the wide range of stages in prophecy, extending to the highest rung, and also to the lowest. The possible varieties of prophecy along the way are as many as the possibilities of interaction between the infinite and the finite.

But above all, let us not forget what the Torah itself says to those who desire to see into the future: "thou shalt be whole-hearted with the L-rd thy G-d" and Rashi explains: "walk with Him wholeheartedly, have faith in Him, seek not to foretell the future but accept whatever comes to you with a full heart, then you will be with Him and you will be His heritage (Deut. 18,13).

8. STRUGGLE TO EXCEL

The Kabbalists teach us that the laws and practices of the Jewish religion have two aspects: the revealed and the hidden. The revealed side (טעם נגלה) of the origin of sin can be illustrated with the comment of Rav (בראשית רבה מ״ד): "Of what importance is it to the L-rd whether meat is eaten without the command of Shechita being performed beforehand? The mitzvot were given to Israel only to refine and improve mankind."

The hidden side (טעם נסתר) of the origin of sin is discussed by the eminent Kabbalist Rabbi Joseph Gikatilia in his comment (סוד הנחש ומשפטיה): "Know that every Divine creation which is located at the place that was designed for it at the time of creation is good. If it leaves that place, it is evil. Thus, it says: "He makes peace and creates evil."

This comes back to the idea of the spheres of creation which we have mentioned in previous chapters. Universal harmony was set in an extremely precise fashion. Every element has its designated place which it must keep or be held responsible for causing great disorder in the system. It is up to mankind to keep the order of the universe, and correct any disturbances resulting from unauthorized changes in position.

In this light we catch a glimpse of the secret meaning of sin and its punishment. Every sin draws a punishment whether committed intentionally or unintentionally (תנחומה הישן ויקרא ט״ו). A person may find it difficult to understand why he ought to atone for a sin committed unconsciously, but it is a different matter from the viewpoint of eternity. The good or bad intentions of the individual do not change the fact that the deed has been done; the crime has been committed and the resulting disturbances in the plan of creation must be corrected.

The Kabbalists chose a special term for the significance of sin in terms of its secret aspect. This term is "קוצץ בנטיעות," which means to cut the young shoots from the stem of a plant. This expression helps the sinner understand that his sin is not only an insult to G-d but also a defiant challenge to universal harmony. Sin is not just a "matter of religion," it is an act which damages creation. This is most serious, for it is the creation of G-d which is the target.

Rabbi Yehudah Chayyat devoted an entire chapter (מערכת אלקות) to questions regarding the principle of "קוצץ בנטיעות." In this chapter he refers to sinners as destructive people, as those who want to destroy the Harmony. He points out that the name "Destroyer of Harmony" was used against Adam at the first sin.

Rabbi Yehuda Chayyat probed further into the wrongdoing committed in the first sin. Adam stood before two trees whose fruits were forbidden to him—"the tree of life in the midst of the garden, and the tree of knowledge of good and evil." The two trees represented the law that man had to obey. They foretold the two aspects to the Divine law: the written (תורה שבכתב) and the oral Torah (תורה שבעל פה).

The first tree, the tree of life, represented the written Torah which contains the laws for an ideal life and which promises man eternal life in the world to come. The second tree, the tree of knowledge of good and evil, represented the oral Torah with its focus on the problems and weaknesses of earthly life.

Adam did not violate the Divine command relating to the ideal life. He held it sacred because he could easily understand that laws pertaining to the ideal are themselves perfect and valid. However, he questioned the Divine command relating to the considerations of earthly life where he felt himself on home ground and not in need of Divine Guidance. He thus became a "קוצץ בנטיעות," a destroyer of the pre-established harmony.

Sin leads to sin and to the serious consequences of sin, which spill over beyond the life of the individual. Just as there is a force of attraction towards the beautiful and the noble, there is another force which demoniacally draws man down towards brutishness and evil. The first generation did not have the strength to withstand this negative onrush, so both man and nature degenerated. They gradually lost the vital energy of their origins. The world tottered in a series of catastrophes and finally collapsed in the dramatic episode of the flood.

Lost in darkness, humanity strove to find its way.

9. TIKKUN—RESTORATION

If we go back to the source of most of the conflicts and antagonisms that have marred the history of humanity, we come to realize that disagreements over the nature of G-d is what divides men. If there were a consensus of what is the highest ideal to which man should give his loyalty, the world would live in peace.

Thus, the kabbalists taught the importance of Tikkun (restoration) to repair the wrongs and offenses committed on earth and restore the unification of G-d. This is expressed as "לשם יחוד קב״ה ושכינתיה." "for the unification of G-d with his Shechina." Here we may think of *Shechina* as the manifestation of G-d, that is, the way G-d is sensed and understood by mankind.

The unification which Tikkun is to bring about leads to brotherhood among all men in universal acceptance of G-d's reign over the entire world.

In the world of human thought and experience we find many apparent opposites, such as matter and spirit, infinite and finite, essence and appearance, joy and anguish, grandeur and decadence, life and death. In each of these relations there is always a positive pole and a negative pole, in the same way that we find a pattern of positive and negative poles throughout the ten Sefirot. The pairings of positive and negative Sefirot (reason and intelligence, justice and love, form and energy) are considered to be a combination of a masculine side and a feminine side. It is important that each factor be "restored to its place" according to the order of the ten Sefirot of universal harmony.

But there is also a middle axis in the pattern of ten Sefirot which holds the fruit of the union of each pair of opposites. As one goes toward the source, the three axis (right, left, and middle) come together and finally blend into a rich and productive unity. It is from this unity that the divine light of Monotheism (knowledge of One G-d) radiates throughout the world.

When men finally reach the stage where they can see that light, they will have restored and readied the world for the rule of G-d, as we say in our prayer of Alenu "לתקן עולם במלכות ש-די", to restore the world to the kingdom of the Almighty."

To whom falls the primary responsibility for bringing about universal Tikkun? Maimonides writes that Christianity and Islam have shown the way for the coming redemption. Many of our Sages adopted a similar positive attitude to these religions. Nevertheless, the great task of Tikkun is not figured among the responsibilities of the non-Jewish peoples (הלכות מלכים בלי צנזור).

Their role is to build great civilizations along the lines laid down in the "Covenant with G-d". The duties of the non-Jewish peoples are reflected in the seven Noachian commandments.

The Zohar tells of a formal call to the children of Israel to take the necessary steps for Tikkun but they needed to be given the means to do so. The Zohar explains that this means is none other than the totality of Mitzvos. Therefore, many of the children of Israel express their purpose in words before performing each Mitzva. They do this by reciting the words "לשם יחוד ... בדחילו ורחימו," thereby expressing the love and fear of G-d which are intermingled in the fulfillment of His will, for the purpose of Tikkun (נפש החיים פרק כ"ח, ל"ד).

How can one explain the influence that the Jews have had on other nations to advance the goal of universal Tikkun?

Israel is not only the keeper and representative of the Divine Law but also its defender and broadcaster. The mission of Israel is to help man recognize the Law so that the kingdom of G-d can be established on earth.

To win men over to the revealed truths, Israel has not resorted to bloody holy wars nor to missionizing and preaching among primitive peoples. Israel has also not indulged in inquisitions or forced conversions. It has been solely through the irresistible power of truth that Israel has succeeded over the centuries in leading humanity to share a large part of its concepts. Israel has thus become the greatest, most efficient missionary the world has ever known. Because its influence has been on such a universal scale, Israel has been fulfilling its noble mission without any systematic search for converts or spectacular cases of individual conversions.

Judaism's great principles continue to exert their power over men. After initiating the idea of monotheism, Israel gave man the idea of unbiased justice, an ideal which mankind has been trying to establish for centuries, amid wars and revolutions. And Judaism's mission is far from over. Judaism still possesses great treasures of truth that humanity has yet to share. These treasures include the concepts of universal harmony discussed in these pages.

Israel's missionary method has also served to protect its national genius from external harm. Because its influence is based solely on the self-evident truth of its example, not on direct personal action, Israel is not required to mix into other nations to spread its ideals. Thus, Israel need not expose itself to foreign influences harmful to its own character. On the contrary, it is by remaining true to itself, its truths and its principles that Israel is best able to accomplish its mission.

Israel follows the example of the Creator Himself. Just as G-d concentrated His Being through the act of Tsimtsum in order to give life to mankind, so Israel is reduced to a small minority in order to give mankind eternal life.

10. THE WORLD'S SPIRITUAL ORIGIN

One of the primary ideas of our religion is that this material world originates from the spiritual. Because G-d is conceived in our minds as spiritual and because He existed before creation, all matter must have been created from the spirit.

The Jew does not fail to refer to this principle whenever he mentions the name of G-d, הקדש ברוך הוא. The first word tells that G-d is קדש, holy, His essence is beyond all that is material. The remaining two words ברוך הוא, "Blessed be He," are a wish that G-d, the source of all blessing be blessed, that is, that He will be a continuing and inexhaustible supply of blessing to mankind.

The blessing which we say before each mitzvah is explained by Nachmanides in his commentary to the book of Exodus (26-15). The blessing begins by speaking directly to the L-rd ("ברוך אתה, Blessed are you") and then continues indirectly in the third person ("אשר קדשנו במצותיו, Who has commanded us with His mitzvos"). The direct forms of address covers the apparent aspects of G-d that we can see and understand in the world around us. The indirect form covers the spiritual aspects that are beyond our normal understanding. Our Sages made a point of emphasizing this lesson of the direct and indirect forms by including them in every blessing. They felt it important to combat that inclination of people to assume and to teach that nothing counts beyond the confines of matter (נפש החיים שער ב, פרק ג, ד).

By expressing his thankfulness for all blessings—spiritual and material—the Jew constantly reminds himself of the spiritual Source of holiness from Whom life and blessing spring. "ישלח עזרך מקדש, He sends you help from (the place of) holiness" (תהלים כ, ג)

11. THE MEANINGS BEHIND THE MITZVOS

There are those who have discouraged the search for the meanings behind the commandments which G-d gave to Israel. Maimonides disagreed strongly with them (Guide 3:31) but summed up their reasoning as follows: If the laws were commanded to us for particular reasons, one could claim that they originated in the thoughts of some very intelligent human being. On the other hand, if an action has no comprehensible meaning and gives no benefit to the person who does it, then this action comes from G-d, because no human thought would lead to such a thing.

Maimonides disagreed with this argument, saying that it leads to the unacceptable conclusion that man is more perfect than his Creator. For this argument would lead us to say that while man speaks and acts with a certain goal in mind, G-d would command us to do that which is of no value to us and forbid us to do that which is harmless. On the contrary, Maimonides tells us, G-d always has our welfare in view. Is it not written, "For our good always, that He might keep us alive (Deut 6,24)? The Torah clearly expects that every one of its statutes will be seen by the nations as coming from wisdom and understanding.

Yet since the Torah itself does not generally provide the reasons behind the various mitzvos, there is always the danger that in assigning meanings to them we might be mistaken and we might even be led to revise them as conditions change and our reasons no longer apply. In fact, the Tur Yoreh Deah states (יורה דעה קפ"א), "We need not seek reasons for the Mitzvos for they are like decrees from the King, even if we do not know their meaning."

In his Iggeres Hakodesh, Rabbi Shneur Zalman of Lyadi, the author of the Tanya, arrives at the same general conclusion. Yet Rabbi Shapiro of Dinov did formulate a system for explaining the Mitzvos and published it under the title: "The Way of Your Mitzvos, דרך פקודיך." Likewise, the famous ספר החינוך.

In discussing the reasons for Mitzvos, the kabbalists distinguished between various approaches to truth: פשט, דרוש, רמז, and סוד, as described in Section 6 of Part I. They considered the first three approaches as various degrees of relative truth, the ultimate absolute truth being סוד. In effect, the great truths are also sheltered in an act of Tsimtsum. One day the pure, secret truth will emerge and the veils of *"Hester Ponim"* will be removed. The Zohar states: To discover the essence of the idea, one must strip the Mitzvah of everything that covers it and go forward on the road to its soul. Once there, one must start again, this time to seek the soul within the soul "נשמה בנשמה." This investigation is just as necessary for the narrative story-telling part of the Torah as it is for the Halachic, legal part. Every word and every letter have their deep significance. The search for this ultimate truth is what should inspire us.

The Zohar uses a beautiful allegory to give us a special insight into the four approaches to truth, the four interpretations of the Torah (Zohar II:99 a-b). The Torah is compared to a beautiful maiden who stays hidden in an isolated chamber of the palace. She has one lover whom no one else knows. Out of love for her he is continually waiting by the door of the palace looking for her in every direction. She knows he is there, but does not come out for she must preserve the secret of their special relationship.

What does she do? She opens a small window in her secret chamber and for a moment reveals her face to her lover, and then quickly hides again. Anyone passing by would see nothing. Only he sees her and his heart and soul are drawn to her. He is aware that out of love for him she has revealed herself to him for that moment.

So it is with the Torah. The Torah reveals itself to those who love it. The man who devotes every day to seeking the Torah, studying its פשט will one day receive a sign, a momentary insight into the Torah's beauty. But it is only for a moment. If through thoughtlessness he misses the signal, the Torah will call him, saying "מי פתי יסור הנה, Let the one who is thoughtless come here" (Prov. 9:4).

As he approaches, the Torah speaks to him words of intelligence, and he enters. This is called דרש. As though from behind a veil, the Torah now tells him words of allegory called הגדה. This is the stage of רמז. Only then after he becomes intimate with the Torah does it speak to him of its secret ways, סוד. He is then called "חתן תורה, bridegroom of the Torah." The Torah tells him, "Now you see that in the first sign I gave you there were so many hidden meanings and secrets. Now you see the truth." Only then does the true literal meaning of the Torah, such as it really is, become clear to him, with its literal text in which not one word can be added or removed.

It would take more than one book to interpret all the precepts of the Torah along the lines of Kabbalah. That objective goes far beyond the purpose of this work. We will therefore limit ourselves to a discussion of a few examples.

Discovering the hidden truth that lies behind external appearances is like discovering the soul deep within the body. To extract the root of a Mitzvah from its covering, one must keep in mind the principle that the Torah does not present ideas in the abstract, but uses a combination of practical examples and symbolic forms. For example, the idea that meat and milk may not be eaten together is expressed by the verse, "you shall not cook a lamb in the milk of its mother" (שמות כ״ג, י״ט).

In our search for סוד we must also not lose sight of the other three interpretations, פשט, רמז, and דרוש. Even the best and most meaningful analysis of a Mitzvah could never change the Halachic requirements for that Mitzvah as set down in the Shulchan Aruch. These words at the beginning of the Bible serve as a teaching for all generations: "And a river comes out of Eden to water the garden; from there it splits into four parts" (Gen 2:10). These four streams represent the ways of interpreting the Torah, פשט, רמז, דרוש, and סוד. Their flows originate from a common source in order to water the spiritual garden of mankind.

The Limits of Our Knowledge

Much has been written concerning the meaning behind the mitzvah, "You shall not take the mother bird with the young" (Deut 22: 6-7). For the Kabbalist approach to this mitzvah, we turn to Racanti. In his ספר טעמי המצוות, he tells us that the "hidden side" of this mitzvah is expressed by a midrash from the Sefer Habahir in which Rabbi Rahumai asks why the father bird is not included in this mitzvah. The answer is given that the mother signifies the source of the world and her young correspond to the seven days of creation.

This midrash wants to teach that there is a limit to our knowledge. "Do not take the mother" means, "Do not try to fathom the secret of the origin of the world." Since you cannot conceive of anything beyond this world, such thoughts can only lead to turning away from the Torah. On the other hand, the children—the seven days of creation—take for yourself. Only within the framework of creation will you be able to elevate your thoughts and discover the heavenly Creator. As the verse in Deuteronomy concludes, the reward for disciplining your thoughts will be that "you will be happy and your days will be prolonged."

Another verse in Deuteronomy states: "The secret things belong to the L-rd" (Deut. 29:28). The Zohar interprets this verse by telling of a conversation between Rabbi Abbah and Rabbi Judah who were walking together. Rabbi Abbah raised an unusually daring question. He asked: "There is one thing I would like to know. Since G-d knew that man would sin and that death would be imposed on him, why did He create him? The Torah preceded this world by 2000 years. In it there are all kinds of descriptions of the death of people. Why then was man created in this world? Man will die whether or not he devotes himself to the study of the Torah. The difference will be seen in the world to come, but here the same fate awaits the righteous and the sinner."

Rabbi Judah answered him by saying: "What is the use of your trying to penetrate the ways of your Master? Whatever you have the right to know, you may question, but if you try to grasp what you do not have the right to know, you will lose your mind."

But Rabbi Abba persisted: "If that is so, then the whole Torah is full of secrets. The Torah is filled with the holy Name of G-d so that whoever studies it is like someone who studies the holy Name.

Therefore shouldn't we be forbidden from asking questions and studying the Torah in depth?" To this, Rabbi Judah replied: "The entire Torah is partly secret and partly open (נסתר ונגלה) and so is the holy Name. We have the right to study and delve into what is open to us but as for what is secret, the secret things belong unto the L-rd our G-d."

Ritual Purification of Levi'im

In the Torah we find that before the Levi'im (Levites) were charged with their new responsibilities in the Temple service, they were required to go through a ritual of purification (Num. 8:7). A central feature of this procedure was the requirement to remove all body hair using a razor.

The Zohar's explanation of this *mitzvah* is based on the fundamental difference between the Kohanim (Priests) and the Levi'im. The Kohanim are identified with the *sefira* of חסד (love), whereas the Levi'im are identified with the *sefira* of דין (justice). In this case, חסד is represented by a majestic beard, whereas the harsh demands of דין are represented by the removal of the protective hair and exposure of the bare skin in the ritual of purification.

The Zohar notes that when Korah saw Aaron and the dignity that his long, white beard gave him, זקן אהרן שיורד (תהלים קל"ג), while he himself was completely shaven, he was overcome with jealousy and began to instigate his rebellion. After all only Aaron had the title of honor לאיש חסידך (דברים ל"ג, ח).

The Levi'im from the side of דין, were the ones who executed the Divine punishment against those who committed the sin of the golden calf. Justice demanded that they take no pity on parents, brothers, or children (Deut. 33:9). Less than a year had passed since that bloody episode and now the Levi'im were to assume a new responsibility of service in the Temple. It was therefore necessary to renew them and so to shield them from the revenge which might have been instigated by their harsh, but necessary actions. This renewal or transformation was expressed by shaving their entire body and bringing their own sin-offerings. The effect of this procedure was an act of טהרה, purification.

Purification is an act of self-improvement accomplished by removing impurities. This is associated with Levi'im. In contrast, sanctification is associated with Kohanim. This is an act of self-improvement accomplished by adding a degree of holiness. To the Kohanim this extra ingredient is symbolized by the beard added to the underlying skin, since their essence is חסד, the beard extends as it were additional חסד, thus called קדושה (holiness). To the Levi'im, the same beard symbolizes the expansion of harshness because דין is their nature which must be stripped away before טהרה can be achieved by shaving all their body hair with a razor.

Forbidden Foods

The first instruction that man received after the flood was the permission to eat meat: "Every moving thing that lives shall be for you to eat" (Gen. 9:3). The fact that the moral reform of mankind began with a "dietary law" shows the fundamental importance given to man's control over what he eats.

For the first 1656 years of creation, mankind had been restricted to a vegetarian diet. Far from calming man's behavior, that diet had allowed him to become cruel, selfish, and perverted. And so the new era beginning after the flood needed a new approach. This involved a new method of moral training so that all of creation would progressively raise itself to holiness.

To better understand the significance of food to man's moral values, we shall begin with chapter 29 in Psalms describing the whole universe like a temple where all sing the glory of G-d. Rabbi M. Cordovero explained this by saying that at every rung of the ladder of creation starting with the lowest forms of life on earth and extending to the highest regions of the spirit, there is a natural reaching upwards and striving to come ever closer to the divine source of life and blessing. (פרדס שער כ״ד, פרק י). In fact, Rabbi Cordovero wrote, the bottom of the ladder extends downward beyond living creatures to organic and inorganic matter. Each level is distinguished by the measure of vitality which it receives from the supreme source of the divine light. The sequential relationship between the levels of creation covers the mineral, vegetable, animal, and human realms.

As described by Rabbi Cordovero, each element of creation continues to rise step by step. Rain falls on the earth and helps the seed to germinate and take root. The seed absorbs matter from the earth and transforms it into vegetable material as it grows into a plant. The plant is eaten by an animal thereby bringing it to a level of existence at which it can be converted to the animal life force, the physical soul (נפש). Ultimately, man eats the flesh of the animal. In becoming part of man's body, the animal is brought closer to the source of light contained in man's spiritual soul (נשמה). In this way, the permission to eat meat is part of the universal uplifting of the elements of nature to the spiritual world where the unchained human soul finally rejoins the heavenly sphere of absolute holiness.

However, the permission to eat meat was not in effect before the flood. As explained by Rabbi Yitzchak Luria, this is because at creation's beginnings, the divine plan was for holiness to spread downward from its divine source to the lowly earth. However, the corruption of the animal world that occurred in Noah's generation blocked the clear path of the downward radiation. Thus, when Noah came out of the ark, he offered a sacrifice to serve as a symbol of consecration for the entire animal species. Holiness would now have to be reached by a much more difficult path, climbing step-by-step upwards from the depths, past all levels of creation.

We have seen that a change in human diet was an essential part of the profound changes which occurred in the moral development of mankind at this dawn of a new era in human history.

Another example of the Kabbalistic approach to forbidden foods is the restriction on the eating of the sciatic nerve in the thigh, גיד הנשה (Gen. 32:33). The Zohar related this restriction to the fact that the sciatic nerve is closely associated with the genital organs. If not controlled, these organs can be the source of man's impure desires, his יצר הרע. And so eating this nerve has the effect of attracting the forces of impurity towards man. The Torah calls it גיד הנשה, where the word הנשה is derived from the verb נשה, to forget. When man eats it, he is drawn to forget himself and to forget his obligations to G-d. (רקאנטי שם).

Esav's spirit discovered that Ya'akov was strong in combat and that his whole body was invulnerable. The only weak point that he could find was the region of the genital organs. And often in the history of Ya'akov's descendants, straying (or "forgetfulness") in the domain of sexual morality remained the weak point by which their enemies could hurt them. An example is the debauchery involving the Jews and the daughters of Moav, which resulted in an appalling number of deaths (Num. chapt. 25). Another example involved "the foreign wives who turned the heart of (King) Solomon towards strange gods" (I Kings 11:4). That eventually led to the separation of the kingdom of Judah. Yet another example was the "mingling with the daughters of the Canaanite peoples" in Ezra's time—again the cause of many misfortunes (Ezra 9:3).

Thus, the prohibition of eating the sciatic nerve is intended to protect the children of Israel from being overcome by the forces of impurity which are at the root of moral and national corruption.

We find the prohibition against the mixing of meat and dairy foods in the verses: "You shall not cook a kid in its mother's milk. Behold, I send an angel to protect you." (Ex. 23:19-20) To explain the connection between these two verses, the Zohar points out that mother's milk represents the source of human wisdom and reason. This must not be disturbed by mixing it with a foreign element.

To help us understand the special meaning of the word "kid גדי," the Torah uses it as a symbol of the wicked Esav, עשו הרשע. When Ya'akov wished to appear as Esav, he put the skin of the גדיי עזים on his hands and neck (Gen. 27:16). Beware, the Torah is telling us, do not bring any foreign elements, such as the kid, the mark of Esav, into our spiritual heritage, which is the "alma mater," the mother giving nourishment to our lives. The Torah goes on to say that such a mixture will estrange us from our covenant with G-d. The first evidence of this will be that instead of protecting us Himself, He will "send His angel." The intrusion of a third element into the intimacy of the covenant is an immediate reaction to Israel's bringing an external element into the spirit of the covenant.

The Lifetime of the World

Will the world last forever? Maimonides taught that although created by G-d, the world is eternal and without end (הלכות תשובה פרק ח הלכה ח). In support of his view Maimonides referred to the words of David and Solomon is such verses as "והארץ לעולם עומדת, The world is maintained forever." Maimonides felt that this view represented the thinking of the Masters in the Mishnah and the Talmud.

However, Nachmanides disagreed with Maimonides. He pointed out that Jewish tradition forsees the self-destruction of the world and a new beginning. He referred especially to the teaching of our Sages that human history unfolds in three parts of 2000 years each, to be followed by 1000 years of the Messianic era—"totally Shabbos and eternal peace" (פרק חלק). The teaching of Nachmanides is supported by the statement which we repeat every day in the morning prayers: "ואחרי ככלות הכל, after everything will have ended, the L-rd will still reign in His grandeur."

Nachmanides related the cycle of the world's life to that of the seven cycles of Shemitta years ending with the 50th year Jubilee (יובל). The Kabbalists clarified this view further; The 7000 years of the world's life cycle correspond to the sequence of the lower seven *sefiros* from חסד to מלכות. These seven *sefiros* are called "ספירות הבנין, the foundation *sefiros*" because they serve as the basis for the three higher, purely spiritual *sefiros*, חכמה, כתר, and בינה.

The special significance of the number 7 in the seven foundation *sefiros* is reflected in the seven days of the week, the seven festival days, the seven weeks between Pesach and *Shavous*, etc. Further details of the meaning of the historical unfolding of the seven *sefiros* can be found in the prayers we say during the seven הקפות on *Hoshanah Rabba*, the seventh day of *Sukkos*.

The cycle of 7000 years ends with the *sefira* מלכות, which is also the *sefira* of the Sabbath, that is, the *sefira* of rest and calm and the *sefira* of the triumphal majesty of the Messiah. Life comes to its fulfilling conclusion in calm and rest. Then, at a new, higher level the world will go on to the next cycle of 7000 years. This cycle will be repeated seven times, until the horn of Jubilee will herald the year 50,000, announcing the returning of the world to its roots (הרמב"ן בשער הגמול).

12 THE RELATIONS BETWEEN ISRAEL AND THE OTHER NATIONS

In Jewish tradition, the number 70 is used to symbolize the number of nations in the world. Thus, the *midrash* tells us that the 70 sacrifices that were brought on the seven days of *Sukkos* were for the benefit of the 70 nations of the world (Rashi on Numbers 29:35). Interestingly, we find this number as a count of the children of Israel in the verse, "כל הנפש לבית יעקב הבאה מצרימה שבעים נפש", All the souls of the House of Jacob that came into Egypt were seventy" (Gen. 46:27). The relationship is not coincidental as Rashi tells us in reference to the verse: "He set the borders of the nations in accordance with the number of the children of Israel" (Deut. 32:8).

Of course, as our Sages in the Talmud noted, the actual count of the family members listed as entering Egypt is only 69 (Bava Basra 123b). Many answers are given to resolve this discrepancy. The answer which is of special interest to us here is that of Rabbi Eliezer who said that G-d Himself joined the 69 members of the family, as it is written: "I shall go down with you to Egypt" (פרקי דר' אלעזר פרק ל"ט). Here we see the Divine Presence (*Shechinah*) as "accompanying Israel in its wanderings among the nations."

We find two other situations where G-d allowed Himself to be included among a number of men in order to save them. One situation is in reference to Abraham's plea for the people of S'dom (Gen. 18:28). As Rashi explains, Abraham first asked for the five towns in the S'dom group to be saved if they contained 50 righteous men, 10 from each town. When G-d agreed to this request, Abraham pressed onward by asking for the towns to be saved if there were only 45, that is, nine from each town. By agreeing to this request also, G-d allowed Himself to be counted as the "tenth man" for the saving of each town.

G-d also allowed Himself to be included among the number of the 10 older sons of Ya'akov during the incident of the selling of Yosef. The Zohar tells that the *Shechinah* hovered over the 10 sons even when they sold Yosef, because they were the nucleus of the Jewish nation. However, R'uven was not present at the actual sale of Yosef. To protect their father from the shock of this knowledge and the calamity which this shock could bring about, the nine brothers pronounced a curse of excommunication if any one of them would reveal the truth. Since R'uven was not present to complete the number ten required for the curse to be valid, G-d allowed Himself to be included as the tenth (Rashi on Gen. 37:33). He did this for the purpose of saving Ya'akov and the future of Israel. Thus, it is to G-d who showed his concern for Ya'akov that the Psalmist turns when he proclaims: "May *Hashem* answer you in the day of distress, may the name of the G-d of Ya'akov protect you" (Psalms 20:2).

It is significant that the Torah mentions the number 70 even though the make-up of this total is not obvious and needs an explanation. This brings to mind the similar cases of 613 for the number of the *mitzvos* and 39 for the number of activities forbidden on *Shabbos*. In each case, the composition of the number is the subject of much discussion and controversy. The number seems to be not just the sum of the individual occurrences but has a meaning of its own.

Rabbi Bahya studies this question and looks to the ancient sources of the Sefer HaBahir. He bases himself on the verse of Exodus: "And they came to Elim, where there were 12 springs of water and 70 palm trees; and they camped there by the waters" (Exod. 15:27). The 12 springs mentioned in this verse are destined to nourish the 70 palm trees. The same relationship exists in the spiritual dimension between the 12 sons of Ya'akov and the 70 members of Ya'akov's expanded family, and then between Israel and the 70 nations of the world.

We find many references in the works of the Kabbalists to the number 12 and its significance as the basis for the radiation of spiritual values to the universe. Our best analogy to spiritual radiation is the radiation of light and energy from the sun. Because of this radiation, the sun affects the structure of our existence. Hence, the number 12 corresponds to the 12 signs of the zodiac which match the 12 months of the solar year. The number 12 lends itself to a natural arrangement of four groupings of three. Thus, the 12 months are grouped in four seasons of three months each.

In fact, the pattern of outward radiation symbolized by the number 12 is based on the number 4 which represents the four directions of the compass. In his vision of the Divine chariot, Ezekiel describes the chariot as being upheld by four angels. The Divine chariot symbolizes the cosmic source from which the vital forces are spread throughout the world (רבינו בחיי במדבר ב). In a reflection of the upper world on earth, we find the camp of the children of Israel at whose center stands the holy Ark. The Ark was patterned after the heavenly chariot over which hovered the Divine Majesty. The camp was organized in the form of a four-sided figure; at each of its sides were grouped three tribes, making the total of 12. From this camp the rays of spiritual radiation spread to the nations of the world, bringing them their source of inspiration.

And so we see in the relationship between the 12 sons and the 70 descendants of Ya'akov the pattern for the spiritual history of the world. Just as Israel goes down into Egypt and begins the long journey across the centuries and the nations, we see the formation of the numerical relationship which reminds them of their eternal mission in history.

The Zohar teaches that among the many mysteries connected with the sacrifices, there is one that involves the square shape of the מזבח (altar) and the vision of the heavenly Throne, spoken of in the book of Daniel (chap. 7). The earthly altar is the reflection of the heavenly Throne. The animals offered upon it, their blood being sprinkled at its four corners, symbolically represent the four wild misshapen animal-like figures that Daniel describes.

According to R. Saadiah Gaon, Daniel had a vision of the four kingdoms—Babylonia, Medea-Persia, Greece, and Rome—that subjugated Israel. These four kingdoms are symbolized by the four animal-like figures in the prophecy: One day they will be sacrificed and of them will remain no more than flesh to be consumed.

But what is the role of the man-like shapes in the vision of Daniel? Perhaps it refers to the martyrs of Israel, the people who gave up their lives throughout its history. In the blessing of רצה in the *Sh'moneh Esrey* prayer, the words "please look with favor upon the sacrifices of Israel and their prayers," are interpreted by Tos'fos (מנחות ק"י, א) as referring to the offerings taken from among the righteous in Israel and placed by the angel Michael upon the heavenly altar. May the L-rd accept these sacrifices favorably (... ואשי ישראל תקבל ברצון). These sacrifices counterbalance the savagery of the oppressors, the kingdoms symbolized by the four wild animals.

13. HOLINESS

It is with deep emotion that we now come to discuss the *mitzvah* of קדושה, to become holy. Of all the tasks that Israel has to perform, the task of holiness is the mot sublime.

From the beginning, Israel's mission was to be a "kingdom of priests and a holy nation" (שמות י"ט, ו). The way to reach holiness is told to us in a passage in the Torah that we repeat twice a day in our

PART III
TO REDEMPTION

By obeying these commands, the Jews became the most sober and prudent people on earth, reserved in all things, and giving in to none of the excesses which degrade man and drag him below the level of the animal. Jewish children learn early to moderate their desires and conquer their urges—to make mind triumph over matter.

And so a perfect state of equilibrium is achieved. The body, remaining pure and vigorous, becomes the best ally of the mind. The mind is enabled to think clearly and rise to the heights of spiritual reflection. And these results are due to the sacrifices of flesh and blood that the Jew has brought to the holy altar, represented by his dinner table. In this sense, the "sacrifices of flesh and blood" refer to his giving up the flesh of prohibited animals and his removing the last traces of blood through ritual slaughter and salting of meat.

Harmony With the Body's Instinct of Reproduction

Man was created in the image of G-d. To honor and support that resemblance, man is expected to preserve his own dignity and self-respect. The problem is how to do this in the face of the allurements and passions of life.

It is very rare to find someone whose heart is sealed and protected from temptations and evil desires. And the truth is that Judaism does not encourage a person to detach himself from the material satisfactions of existence or to violently curb his senses. To do this would exile him from society and make him useless to his fellow man.

On the other hand, to satisfy all his sensual appetites would have even more disastrous effects. It would degrade him, transform him into a brute, and stifle the stirrings of his Divine soul.

Judaism seeks to give its children the means to make the best use of their instincts. In the practice of their faith, Jews are able to enjoy life's pleasures without sacrificing their souls and their greatness among the beings of creation. This result is brought about by a series of *mitzvos* which accompany the Jew throughout his life, starting almost as soon as he is born.

The first is the law of circumcision—a permanent sign to remind the Jew that sensual passions are to be controlled. Sexual instincts must be prevented from reaching such an intensity that they dominate life. Only eight days after entering the world, the Jew finds himself committed to taking the path of self-control. The sacrifice of blood at the threshold of his life becomes a highly significant act to seal the sacred covenant between the Jew and G-d. Before this moment, the genital area was identified only with unclean and socially unacceptable acts. Now, through the *mitzvah* of circumcision, it receives the seal of the divine and becomes an essential part of man's spiritual elevation.

However, the conflict between flesh and spirit cannot be resolved in a single step. The solution must come from a long, patient, and consistent training. Even before a child enters the world, his parents establish the framework for that training by bringing their own relationship and their way of life to a high level of moral purity. The influence of this care and love, together with that of previous generations of parents and grandparents, is carried right to their children through the natural process of heredity.

In this progressive training, circumcision represents only the first stage in the development of the individual. It is followed by the long series of *mitzvos* and customs which are so essential to Jewish upbringing. That upbringing is filled with purity and moral nobility. For example, the young Jew is called upon to abstain from sexual contacts before marriage. Through chastity the young man gains self-mastery and with it, human dignity. He learns to control and neutralize his sexual instincts through absorption in spiritual occupations such as intense study of the Torah.

On the other hand, young people are encouraged to start a home early in life. Through marriage two beings are sanctified for the most sacred goal in life—bringing a new generation into the world to carry on G-d's holy work. Furthermore through marriage, it is possible for two people to share life intimately. The wife becomes "עזר כנגדו, the helpmate" by her husband's side, giving him the fulfillment that he in turn gives to her. The young couple help to complete each other's physical, psychological, and social development.

Marriage is a divine institution, and only through marriage can man find this "שלימות," completion, in a pure and holy form. Any other form of cohabitation outside of marriage and not governed by its laws is considered an abomination.

In contrast to the special responsibility given to the Jewish man in the learning of Torah, the Jewish woman is given a special responsibility to be the guardian angel and builder of the Jewish family. The great dignity with which the Halacha surrounds the Jewish woman helps her in her role creating an atmosphere of serenity and peacefulness in the home. This atmosphere depends on the shared love and respect between husband and wife as it does between parent and child.

The structure of Halacha concerning the family is crowned by the "טהרת המשפחה, the laws of family purity." Their purpose is to regulate the sexual relations of the couple so that they will help rather than hinder the fulfillment of a good marriage. These Halochos serve to create the most favorable conditions for conception of new life. They guard against the great dangers that lie in wait to harm marital love: excess and routine. Furthermore, they bring the divine ray of holiness even into the areas of purely physical love.

The reference point is the natural phenomenon of the woman's menstrual period. From the onset of this period relations between husband and wife are forbidden by the verse in Leviticus "ואל אשה בנדת טמאתה לא תקרב, You shall not come near the woman in the time of her impure flow" (Lev. 18:19). Relations remain forbidden even beyond this period, for a total of 12 days in all. The menstrual flow is treated as a time in which the woman's body renews itself and goes through a process of physical and spiritual purification, culminating in a ritual immersion in a purifying bath; "מקוה."

At the end of the 12 days of abstinence and after waiting a period of time identical to the moon's cycle, the wife reappears to her husband as desirable as when she first became his bride. Having conscientiously observed the period of separation, with all the sacrifices that it involves, having surrounded herself with a series of ritual precautions and said the sacred words of the blessing, she emerges from the ritual bath feeling not only clean in body but sanctified in body and soul. She feels transformed and wrapped in shining radiance. In this religious rapture of her whole being she goes forward to meet her husband. Such holy preparation cannot fail to have the most favorable influence on the seed that may come to grow within her as the result of the union, blessed by G-d.

Through these practices the conflict between flesh and spirit vanishes. With sexual life regulated to the smallest detail by divine commandments, man cannot debase his body and his soul by immoral or unclean thoughts or acts. "כי ה׳ אלקיך מתהלך בקרב מחנך... והיה מחניך קדוש ולא יראה בך ערות דבר, For the L-rd your G-d walks in the midst of your camp . . . therefore your camp shall be holy" (Deut. 23:15).

To be sure, the twelve-day wait might seem to some quite long. But experience has shown that it establishes a perfect rhythm in the relations between husband and wife, harmonizing exactly between two great needs: to prevent an excess of selfish lust and to prevent the coldness of over-familiarity. Only a religion of divine origin could teach a code of sexual morality that so fully satisfies the most intimate bodily and psychological needs.

Harmony With the Body's Instinct of Self-Preservation

The vital instinct of preservation of the self is the third factor which affects the harmony between flesh and spirit, mind and matter. Is there a conflict between man's ego—his drive for creative action—and his dependence on an all-powerful G-d? If one were to study other religions, one would find a serious conflict indeed, resulting in an unfortunate gap between religion and life. By turning away from man's creative nature in their search for his spirituality, religions are often relegated to the unhappy, the unfortunate, and uneducated to those who are submissive by nature.

But Judaism is different. It perfectly harmonizes the individual's dynamic nature with his dependency as a creature of the world. Indeed it assigns to Jews a task of universal scope which demands at every moment the greatest clarity of mind, stoutness of heart, and energetic action in all areas of life. This task is none other than the creation of the kingdom of G-d on earth. All of Judaism is directed toward this goal. That is why it develops men with unwavering determination and tireless devotion to overcome any obstacles that stand in their way. The religion of Israel is clearly dynamic.

It stimulates clear thinking through the rigorous logic of the Talmud. It stimulates energy through the demanding discipline of its Halacha. It stimulates feeling through the mystical warmth of its customs. It stimulates devotion through its uplifting messianic mission. It stimulates courage through its lesson of survival despite the suffering of countless hardships.

and slaves, nor between friends and enemies. (הלכות רוצח פרק א, הלכה א).

The Law makes man responsible for the soundness of his body and for the safeguarding of his health and his dignity. It forbids him from doing harm to his body, even if that harm consists of self-inflicted cuts or bruises, or shaving his beard with a razor. The respect that is due the body is also seen in the requirements of burial for the dead.

Moreover, it confers upon each human being a natural dignity that preserves from shame even the wrongdoer suffering his punishment. A wrongdoer may be deserving of a punishment of 40 lashes, but the Torah warns the judge not to exceed this penalty, "פן יוסיף להכותו... ונקלה אחיך לעיניך, that your brother should not be dishonored before your eyes'' (Deut. 25:3). Even the body of a person sentenced to death for his crimes must be given consideration, "לא תלין נבלתו על העץ כי קבור תקברנו ביום ההוא כי קללת אלקים תלוי, his body shall not remain on the scaffold all night but you shall bury him the same day, for he that is hanged is a reproach to G-d'' (Deut. 21:23).

Individual Freedom

Another example of the principle of justice in Judaism relates to individual freedom. The Law assures employees that their rights will be protected. It requires that the contract of employment be for a fixed period. The Torah emphasizes that men are intended to be servants of G-d rather than other men, "כי לי בני ישראל עבדים, עבדי הם", For the children of Israel belong to me as servants'' (Lev. 25:55). There exists no reason that is so able to preserve individual freedom. The only ideal in whose name man can struggle to escape from the many forms of dictatorship is the ideal of serving G-d in universal brotherhood. Any other doctrine will inevitably tend to turn men into slaves under a new tyranny after liberating them from the old.

Respect for Private Property

Justice requires that each person respect the property of his fellow. The principle of private property is established in the story of creation: "פרו ורבו ומלאו את הארץ וכבשה ורדו בדגת הים, Be fruitful and multiply, fill the earth and subdue it'' (Gen. 1:28). Through this Divine blessing, G-d gives man the authority to lay claim to the earth's benefits for his individual use. Thus, any violation of the honestly acquired property of another, represents the violation of a formal right consecrated by G-d.

Furthermore, such a violation is an act of defiance against the Creator. The standards of justice are founded upon an inalienable right instituted by G-d Himself. This is a right that offers absolute guarantees in contrast to the grounds that simple human reasoning might offer (occupation, inheritance, natural law, social expediency).

The same aspect of universality is seen in the question of ownership of land. The land is not the property of the society or of the nation. G-d says, "כי לי הארץ כי גרים ותושבים אתם עמדי, The land is Mine, for you are like strangers and settlers with Me" (Lev. 25:23). Having created the land, G-d distributed it to men "לעבדה ולשמרה, to cultivate it and to guard it" (Gen. 2:15). Consequently they do not receive permanent ownership of property but only temporary possession of it so that they may enjoy its produce. They can sell their land only for a specific number of years—by law the land returns to them and their descendants in the Jubilee year. This principle puts real estate on an established footing. It always returns to the family, thereby preventing the abuses of feudalism or capitalist exploitation.

Judicial Procedures

The purpose of Jewish judicial procedures is to seek the truth of the case. This search is not to be distorted by rituals or even considerations of social welfare. At judicial hearings, the procedures are public and direct, without intermediaries between the judge and the parties involved. In this spirit Moses said: "ושפטתי בין איש ובין רעהו והודעתי את חקי הא׳...ואת תורותיו, When they have a matter and bring it to me, I judge between a man and his neighbor and I make known the judgement of G-d and His laws" (Ex. 18:16).

Form never overrides content, as it did in the process of Roman law. Accordingly, the parties can appeal in case of an error in their original arguments. In criminal law, the hearings can begin over again four or five times if the condemned person finds new arguments in his favor. If the death penalty has been passed, and if only one of the judges finds an argument strong enough to justify acquittal, the sentence is annulled.

The code of justice is not based on rigid formulas. Each case must be individually judged on its own merits. The judges are not merely passive referees of a courtroom drama but are active participants, using all of their experience and knowledge in searching and questioning so that they can determine the truth.

Justice and the State

Jewish justice is "global," uniformly applied in all situations whether between individuals or governments. In the Jewish conception, the State is founded on the Law because the Law existed before the State.

The Prophet Isaiah proclaimed that the salvation of mankind depends on the application of justice in the workings of the State as well as in the interrelationships between countries: "ציון במשפט תפדה ושביה בצדקה, Zion shall be redeemed with justice and they that return to her by righteousness" (Isaiah 1:27).

When King Zedekiah questioned Jeremiah about how to ensure victory in the war against his enemies, the prophet answered by calling for the strict application of social justice in the nation (Jeremiah 34). Furthermore, the sanctity of treaties between nations appears in the Bible as one of the fundamental principles of international law. When King Saul violated the treaty of friendship with Gibeon the entire nation was punished (2 Sam. 21:1).

Judaism opposes the principle of a double standard of morality which requires a person's public life to be answerable to justice, while permitting one's private life to be left to the value system of the individual. Such inconsistency and hypocrisy lead ultimately to injustice and anarchy.

Justice and Religion

Justice cannot be separated from morality and religion. When Jehoshaphat, king of Judah, appointed new judges, he said to them, "ראו מה אתם עושים כי לא לאדם תשפטו כי לה׳ ... יהי פחד ה׳ עליכם", Consider well what you do, for you do not judge in the name of man, but in the name of the L-rd. Therefore, let the fear of the L-rd be upon you" (2 Chron. 19:6). In reference to these words, Maimonides wrote that the courtroom should always contain Divine Presence. Thus, the judges should sit in the fear of G-d and dressed in a prayer shawl (הלכות סנהדרין פרק ג, הלכה ז).

Maimonides added that anyone who commits a wrong against society sins before G-d. In the days of the Temple in Jerusalem, in some cases one had to bring a sin-offering to G-d after he had received the punishment of his sentence.

The importance of the Divine Presence in judgement is so great that after the destruction of the Temple, the judges were no longer allowed to impose the death penalty. It was felt that only in the full shadow of the Divine Presence could one have the power of life and death over another human being.

Justice and Love

As completely logical as the above description of justice may seem, it is nevertheless missing something important. No one has said it better than Israel's sages in the statement quoted by Rashi on the very first verse of the Torah: "בתחילה עלה במחשבתו לברותו במדה״ד וראה שאין העולם מתקיים, והקדים מדת רחמים ושתפה למדה״ד, In the beginning G-d planned to create the world strictly on the principle of justice, but seeing that the world could not endure, He added to it the principle of love."

Nature offers us the spectacle of a perfect order, ruled by an all-powerful and unchangeable Law. In the human sphere alone is the Law softened by love. Love opens vast horizons to the feelings of goodness, kindness, and generosity which G-d created as part of man's makeup.

An example of the application of love in legal matters is the principle of going "לפנים משורת הדין," beyond the letter of the law," giving up one's full legal rights so that another person may benefit.

For example, we are told in the Talmud (Bava Metzia 35a) that if it happens that a worker must give up his land to pay for damage that he has done, he may reclaim the land whenever he is able to pay. The reason given is: "ועשית הישר והטוב, And you shall do that which is right and good in the eyes of the L-rd" (Deut. 6:18).

In another example, we find the story (Bava Metsia 83a) of some porters who broke a barrel of wine belonging to Rabba, son of Bar Channa. When Rabba took their clothing to pay for the damage, the workers went and complained to Rav. Rav immediatly told Rabba to return the clothing. Rabba was surprised.

"Is that the law?" he asked.

"Yes it is," answered Rav, "as it is said "למען תלך בדרך טובים, that you may walk in the way of good men" (Prov. 2:20).

The story continues that Rabba returned their clothing, but the workers complained to Rav, "we are poor men and have worked all day. Now we are hungry and have nothing to eat."

"Go and pay them," said Rav.

"Is that the law?" asked Rabba.

"Yes it is," he answered, "as is stated (in the same verse) ואורחות צדיקים תשמר, and keep to the path of righteous."

Jewish law is strict and uncompromising in its principles, but it shows itself to be all the kinder and more humane when applied in actual practice. (במדבר ל״ה, כ״ה). The Torah gives us an early example of this when it describes how the death sentence for the first sin was reduced to exile from paradise.

The Sages of Israel followed that example. They practically abolished the death penalty, (מכות ז, א). Moved by the same spirit, they gave a large place to extenuating circumstances in the forming of court decisions.

And although the basic principle of justice is that "punishment shall fit the crime," the Sages interpreted the law of "an eye for an eye" to mean that damage to an eye must be paid in money with an amount equal to the value of an eye.

The Law is never considered the maximum that a person is expected to do. Rather it represents the moral minimum which is already at a high ethical level, but is not enough. The requirement is that the ethics of love and understanding will complete the judicial code. Thus, the code defines the rights of the individual with respect to society; it sets the minimum protection to which each person is entitled. But then the law asks us to go beyond, to open up the inexhaustible supply of good deeds in the human heart, to do what is good—not to remain indifferent to the plight of others.

Jewish social legislation gives a typical example of the relationship between justice and love. It requires that every community set up welfare institutions which are dependent on taxation of property owners. On the other hand, so as not to reduce charity to some mechanical expression of social work, it assigns a leading role to duties of compassion: visiting the sick, burying the dead, comforting the afflicted, hospitality, support of poor newlyweds, protection of orphans and widows, reconciliation of enemies, and so on.

Love crowns the structure of society whose foundations are based on essential justice. In that image is contained the basic principle of social harmony.

3. THE HARMONY OF REASON AND FAITH

People have a tendency to channel their thinking into one of two directions: either they emphasize matters of this world or they stress spiritual matters. Those who choose the first path hold up Reason and Science as the supreme authority. Those who follow the second path turn to Faith and the Mystical.

An emphasis on Reason and Science alone leads to a condition whereby industry and technology rule over society. This "technological paradise" results in a destructive progress, creating a culture eager for comfort and luxury but living under the threat of total annihilation. On the other hand, the second solution focusing on life in the next world leads to superstition and the occult, while neglecting social problems in life in this world.

Judaism discourages us from separating the two ways of thinking and choosing one over the other. Quite the contrary, these two ways of thinking should complement one another and join in a harmonious unity. Faith in G-d and in a world to come prevents man from giving up his soul to rational science and the culture to which it gave birth. Reason, on the other hand, forbids the spirit to lose itself in an unreal and imaginary world.

Judaism rejects neither rationalism or mysticism. It knows that the universe can never be understood in the light of one without the other. The human soul thirsts for both rational and mystical ideas. Each has a place reserved for it in the plan of creation. The rational lays the solid foundation for the life of the individual and for life in society. The mystical brings man into contact with the spiritual source of his existence.

Unity of Thought

Rational thought goes out to meet the non-rational and seeks to unite with it. It tries to embrace the sphere of supernatural power which is continually injecting creativity and originality into the human spirit. The inexhaustible Heavenly source of thought has always been an unshakable principle in the Jew's belief in one G-d.

Unity of thought leads to unity of actions—and, as a result, the unity of all of life, individual and social. To pave the way for unity of thought, Judaism asks us to develop both mind and soul. To reach the discovery of the Infinite; purely intellectual investigation needs to be reinforced by the search in our innermost soul for personal contact with G-d. The entire soul must embrace the Universal Soul and that union depends on perfect harmony in one's emotional and spiritual life.

Development of the Mind through Torah

To develop the mind to reach unity of thought Judaism provides a rigorous and methodical training which places the Torah in the forefront. From the start Judaism chooses a path that is completely different from that of modern civilization. Modern civilization directs a person's thinking to the sciences, leaving it to the individual to discover or ignore the spiritual world beyond his physical surroundings as he wishes. In contrast, Judaism gives priority to the truths revealed by G-d through the Torah.

The Divine spirit is revealed on earth in three ways: Nature, History, and the Divine Word. The first two of these are more heavily veiled than the third. Thus, the study of the natural and sociological sciences may start from positive facts but only rarely leads the student to the threshhold of spiritual awareness. As long as a person's thinking is limited to the closed system of material facts, he tends to consider scientific conclusions as totally free from the possibility of error. He is likely to totally disregard the truths of the spiritual world.

Furthermore, because the areas of research for human logic are necessarily defined within the framework of time and space, they are inevitably limited to ideas within that framework (Maimonides, Guide for the Perplexed I, 31). To gain access to the Infinite, a person needs a reliable guide to the world of existence beyond the physical. That guide is nothing other than the Torah, which remains true today as it was when it was first revealed to the Jewish nation.

The Torah opens up far broader vistas than those of our limited material surroundings. It is a revelation of G-d's spirit that is much more positive and definitive than the other two forms of His revelation —Nature or History. The Torah is the Divine spirit clothed in the garment of the Word. Each of its laws, each of its episodes, each of its words reveal a new aspect of this spirit and deserve to be studied thoroughly in a search for their deepest meaning. Only then can man begin to grasp the mystery of the Universal Soul.

Besides revealing to us the ideas and concepts of the non-material world that the sciences are hardly aware of, the Torah gives us a guide for living. By faithfully following this guide we become conscious of the Supreme Being in a far deeper sense than any intellectual investigation ever could attain.

However, Judaism does not lose sight of the need to harmonize spiritual concepts with rational reasoning. After a thorough grounding in the study of Torah, the student may delve into the natural and historical sciences, always being aware that because of their limitations, they must take second place to revealed truth. In fact, Maimonides refers to them as the "concubines of the Torah" (Iggeret Hateshuva, Brunn edition, p. 40b). Whenever Jews have allowed themselves to reverse the order of importance of these fields of study, they have sunk into the swamp of materialism and have nearly lost their G-d.

Developing Harmony Between Reason and Faith

The development of harmony between reason and faith is a worthy and noble goal for the thinking Jew. It demands a great deal of commitment, far beyond a simple reordering of priorities. In fact, a lifetime plan of rigorous study needs to be followed, directed to a logical and thorough investigation of revealed truths.

The Talmud is a bridge between reason and faith. It provides us with the format for a systematic critical analysis of the truths presented to us in the Torah. This results in an interlocking harmony, wherein the study of spiritual values is subjected to a disciplined application of rational logic while at the same time, reason is placed under the guidance of the revealed truths. This continuous interaction causes a progressive development and adjustment in our understanding so that the apparent conflict between reason and faith eventually vanishes altogether. Reason and faith become fused together as we gain insight into the oneness of universal truth.

Interestingly, the logical method used in the learning of Torah is similar to that used by science. In both cases, one begins by a careful observation and study of detailed facts and then finds the principles or theories which can explain the specific cases. These principles can then be used in future applications. The text of the Torah is the raw material which must be carefully examined and understood. The instruments used to study this material are the 13 rules of Biblical interpretation defined by tradition. The resulting body of detailed facts forms the basis of the Oral Law, the Mishnah and the Talmud. From the individual cases, general principles are derived which are then applied in guiding one's course of action in new situations and in the understanding of the mysteries of existence.

These vast studies extend to all domains of thought and human activity. However, the vision of the Infinite can be extended even more by separating the words and letters of the Torah from their covering of general meaning. G-d has given us in the Torah another dimension of knowledge based on numerical analysis (גמטריא). Within this dimension is hidden the secrets of the structure of the universe. Transported by the rhythm of the poetry of words and phrases, the mind can discover the mysteries of the cosmic spheres in their melodious symphony. At a still higher level, the numbers and the poetry become one in a heavenly harmony, the spirit meeting the original, pure source of prophetic inspiration.

Developing Harmony Between Heart and Mind

The development of the mind cannot proceed without a simultaneous development of the emotions. All our efforts to grasp the supreme truths will fail if we do not give full consideration to the functions of the heart as well as of the mind. It is the rhythmic interaction between these two factors that creates the unity of the human soul.

When man prepares himself to contemplate the divine mysteries, in his heart he hears the same words Moshe heard at the burning bush: "אל תקרב הלם...אדמת קודש הוא, Do not come near to this place for the ground on which you are standing is holy ground!" (Exod. 3:5). And as Moshe did, he will have to "ויסתר משה פניו כי ירא מהביט אל האלקים, hide his face for fear of looking at the L-rd" (Exod. 3:6). To know the Supreme Being, one has to experience intellectual modesty and humility before G-d. "יראת ה' ראשית דעת," The awe of G-d is the beginning of knowledge" (Proverbs 1:7).

Man's thoughts can spring upward to the spheres of higher truth only in the atmosphere created by the prayers and synagogue service that the Torah calls: "ולעבדו בכל לבבכם," the "service of the heart" (Deut. 11:13). The spiritual uplift provided by the Sabbath, the festivals and the many מצות accompanying them transport the soul toward G-d in a fervent glow of the whole personality. Little by little, love and awe blend and their union gives birth to the "שמחה של מצוה, joy of *mitzvah*" in limitless devotion.

Jewish prayers are said from a feeling of love and trust toward G-d the universal Father, the Creator of the world. This feeling is mixed with the awareness of G-d as the supreme Judge. The daily dialogue between these feelings brings the Jew closer to his G-d.

Judah Halevi tells us (Kuzari 3:5) that the moments of prayer form the core and choicest part of a person's time. The other hours are just paths leading to it. The believer looks forward to the time of prayer, because during it he becomes a spiritual being and is removed from his material existence. Just as the Sabbath is the crowning day of the week, so is the time of prayer the crowning time of the day. Prayer is to the soul what nourishment is to the body. The blessing of one prayer lasts till the time of the next, just as each meal gives a person the strength to carry on until the next meal. During prayer a person purifies his soul from the effects of evil or materialism to which he might have been exposed since his last prayer. In this way not a day goes by without his body and soul being completely restored.

The paths of prayer are bordered by *mitzvos*, imprinting Divine thought on all that surrounds us. For example, the *tzitzis* for our clothes, *mezuzos* for our houses, and *tephilin* for our bodies bind universal harmony. That stage lasted from the creation until Abraham. The second stage was dominated by the giving of the Torah to Israel at Mount Sinai and continued until the destruction of the Temple in Jerusalem. The third stage, in which we live, is the one that is preparing the world for Moshiach. The beginning of this stage was marked by the exile of Israel from its land and the spread of the idea of One G-d among the nations. It is continuing for century after century until the seventh thousand-year period, the era of Moshiach.

The era of Moshiach is the one that will be "שכולו שבת ומנוחה לחיי עולמים, totally Shabbos and everlasting peace." Just as each Shabbos already begins on the sixth day, before nightfall, the first signs of Moshiach's time begin to appear even as the sixth thousand-year period draws to a close. However, the actual time of Moshiach's coming, whether sooner or later, remains dependent on Israel's actions according to Psalms (צ״ה) in the verse "היום אם בקולו תשמעו."

It is thus in the third stage of human history that the Kingdom of G-d will be created. It will be achieved first by Israel within itself and then by a drawing together of all mankind. This development must be accomplished gradually, over a period of time involving seven stages, as described below.

First Stage of the Kingdom of G-d

The successive events in the creation of the Kingdom of G-d are identified in our daily prayer, the *sh'mone esrei*. After the blessings concerning personal wishes, the prayer speaks of our wishes for Israel's national future. The sequence is explained by the Talmud (Megilah 17b) and begins with the tenth blessing, "תקע בשופר גדול לחרותנו, Announce our freedom on the great *shofar*." This event involves the ingathering of the exiles to the Promised Land. "וקבצנו יחד מארבע כנפות הארץ, And gather us together from the four corners of the world."

Second Stage of the Kingdom of G-d

The ingathering is expected to take place in peace and with the consent of the other nations. It is associated with a task of supreme importance for the creation of the Kingdom of G-d: the reestablishment of the rule of justice. "ואשיבה שופטיך כבראשונה ויעציך כבתחילה ואחרי כן יקרא לך עיר הצדק קריה נאמנה. ציון במשפט תפדה ושביה בצדקה," And I will restore the judges as in the days of old and your counsellors as at the beginning. Afterward you will be called the city of Justice. Zion will be redeemed by justice and they that return to her by righteousness'' (Isaiah 1:26). Thus, the eleventh blessing begins "השיבה שופטינו כבראשונה ויעצינו כבתחילה, Return our judges as of old and our counsellors as at the beginning.'' The fulfillment of this step is represented by the Sanhedrin, which will be established before the coming of Moshiach (Maimonides, Commentary on the Mishnah, Sanhedrin #1).

Third and Fourth Stages of the Kingdom of G-d

Now come the next two events in the historical development, indicated by the 12th and 13th blessings. From the earliest times, the prophets predicted that the coming of Moshiach will be preceded by an age of "birth pangs" which will take the form of the wars of destruction of Gog and Magog. This verse was described at length by the prophet Yechezkel (chapters 38 and 39) and by the Talmud (Sanh. 97a). The idea behind these events is explained in Tehilim (ע"ה) "וכל קרני רשעים אגדע תרוממנה קרנות צדיק", I will cut off the horns of the wicked but the horns of the righteous shall be lifted up.'' The triumph of good will ultimately require the violent destruction of the enemies of G-d. Thus, the 12th blessing of the *sh'moneh esrei* ends with the words: "שובר אויבים ומכניע זדים, He crushes (His) enemies and subdues the wicked,'' and the 13th belssing ends with the words, "משען ומבטח לצדקים, He is the support and the confidence of the righteous.''

The wars of destruction of Gog and Magog may be understood as part of a historical process which is similar to that of extracting precious metals from raw ore. The process calls for repeated refining operations, each of which involves the selection of the desired materials and the removal of waste materials. This process began with Avrohom, whose child Yitzchok was selected to carry on the Jewish tradition, while his other child, Yishmael, was returned to the mainstream of the nations. The successive operations of concentrating the good also have the effect of concentrating the bad, so that it ultimately becomes necessary to eliminate a people made up of the convinced enemies of G-d, symbolized by Amalek (מכלתא סוף בשלח).

Tradition emphasizes that the reasons for the wars of Gog and Magog are related to the reasons for the wars against Amalek (Brochos 58a). Gog and Magog represent the seventy nations of the world. In fact, the numerical value of גוג ומגוג adds up to 70 (Tanchuma,

Korach). Despite thousands of years of effort to establish truth, there is still a part of humanity that will forever rebel against the cause of G-d. With no other solution remaining, that incorrigible group will have to be blotted out, a necessary sacrifice to the fulfillment of history.

In this light, one can understand the unfolding of history of a world divided into two totally opposed blocs of nations—one for G-d and the other for the enemies of G-d. The antagonism between the two forces will build up until an ulitmate test of strength takes place. This monumental duel, making use of the most destructive weapons of a technological civilization, will draw all of mankind into a series of wars in which Israel, caught between the giants, will almost be crushed. The gigantic cataclysm will bring about the ultimate selection of the righteous, of those faithful to G-d and His word.

Fifth and Sixth Stages of the Kingdom of G-d

Only after this last judgement will Jerusalem be rebuilt, once again to become the Holy City. The Temple will rise up majestically on Mount Zion. Thus, the fourteenth blessing of the *Sh'moneh esrei* begins "ולירושלים עירך ברחמים תשוב, and to Jerusalem your city, return with love."

The Divine Pillar will return to hover over the cherubim on the Holy Ark, making dazzlingly clear to the world that Israel and its G-d have reconciled.

At this time, a glorious kingdom will be set up in Israel under the sceptre of the Moshiach of the House of David. Thus, the fifteenth blessing begins, "את צמח דוד עבדך מהרה תצמיח," And make the seedling of David your servant grow." The nation will be surrounded with the respect and gratitude of the other peoples as it was in the days of the Kingdom of Judah.

Seventh Stage of the Kingdom of G-d

The last stage is the achievement of universal brotherhood, consolidated by the universal worship of G-d, the Father of all mankind. Thus, the embodiment of this ideal is the House of Prayer, as we see from the vision of the Prophet Isaiah, "והביאותים אל הר קדשי ושמחתים בבית תפלתי עולותיהם וזבחיהם לרצון על מזבחי כי ביתי בית תפלה יקרא לכל העמים, I will bring them to my holy mountian, I will fill them with joy in my House of Prayer; their burnt-offerings and their sacrifices will be acceptable upon My altar; for my house shall be called a House of Prayer for all peoples'' (56:7). Thus, the sixteenth blessing of the *sh'moneh esrei*, which is the seventh of the national blessings, ends with the words, ''שומע תפלה, Who hears prayer.'' The prayers of the nations, spoken in universal brotherhood, will be heard and will be answered by the G-d of all mankind.

6. HARMONY BETWEEN ISRAEL AND ITS LAND

A deep mystery seems to surround Israel and its land. The land is not able to bear its inhabitants for long if they are not faithful to their covenant. When they neglect their promise, the land rejects them and delivers them to their enemies.

Every other nation is related to its land simply as a homeland. This feeling is based on sentimental attachments developed over a period of time, living in the land and gradually becoming identified with it.

With Israel, however, the relationship is unique because it is a spiritual one. (דברים י״א, י״ז). Israel was created as a nation long before it took possession of its homeland. Yet that homeland was promised at Israel's birth as a nation. Moreover, that homeland was designated as the indispensable means by which Israel would fulfill its mission as a nation. Because of that special sense of future fulfillment, the land has become the object of our eternal desire, a desire which cannot be satisfied until we embrace the land in perfect harmony.

The land is for Israel what the body is for the soul. Upon emerging from its otherwordly source, the soul seeks a material covering in order to fulfill its earthly destiny. Israel, too, seeks the geographical region that will fit in with its soul as a people. Only the Promised Land offers Israel the three elements that correspond intimately to the three elements of its soul: to Israel's spiritual vitality the land offers the maginficent dignity of the Sanhedrin; to its moral and emotional life the land offers the awesome foundation of the Temple in Jerusalem; and to its national hopes the land offers the seat of the royal dynasty of David.

emptiness carried within it the seeds of rebirth. All of creation seeks to regain its place in the harmony of the universe.

The Return

"מי עור כי אם עבדי", Who is blind but my servant" (Isaiah 42:19).

The children of Israel are like travellers going towards daybreak. They look forward to it as though in a dream without suspecting that at any moment the sun will light up the world. The Zohar explains that for each exile that Israel had to undergo, a time limit was set. However, each time it was up to Israel to return when it was ready. Yet this time is different. As the prophet Amos said, "נפלה לא תוסף קום בתולת ישראל נטשה על אדמתה אין מקימה, The maiden of Israel is fallen and can raise herself no more; she is cast down on her land and there is none to raise her up" (Amos 5:2).

The wording in Amos is not "I will not raise her up," but "she can raise herself up no more." This is like the story of a king who is angry at his queen. He banishes her from the royal palace for a fixed period. When that passes, she returns to the king. This happens again. But when it happens a third time she is sent away for a longer unspecified period.

And so the king says to himself, "This time is not going to be like the other times. This time I must go to her with all the ministers of the palace and ask her to come back." When he comes to where she is living, he finds her cast down in the dust. How much honor is then given to the queen! And how much does the king desire to have her back with him! He takes her by the hand and he raises her up and leads her back to the royal palace. He promises her that he will never again separate from her. Thus did the L-rd. Whenever Israel was in exile it could return to the L-rd. But this time is different. Israel will be cherished and lavished with words of tenderness and love. And that is the meaning of the prophet's words, "ביום ההוא אקים את סוכת דויד הנופלת (עמוס ט, יא), on that day I will raise up the tabernacle of David that is fallen to the earth." It does not state, "It will raise itself up," but "I will raise it up." And what is meant by the "tabernacle of David?" It is the maiden of Israel.

Israel and the Other Nations

In our effort to understand the goal of universal harmony to which Israel is striving, some insight is needed into the pattern of conflict between Israel and the other nations of the world. It is the contrast between the spiritual and material planes that is the cause of the misunderstanding, suspicion, and hostility of the nations toward Israel (רש״י בראשית כ״ה, כ״ב).

The existence of Israel is dependent on a spiritual dimension, without which the nation could not have survived. If Israel as a nation has been able to endure for thousands of years without a land, without a government, and without a common language, it is because Israel is carried by powers of the spirit. This quality distinguishes Israel from other nations who owe their existence to more material considerations such as their roots in their native land, their sense of tribal brotherhood, or their common political ideals.

The absolute belief in one G-d which is the basis of Israel's spiritual value system emphasizes the unity of life on earth through the power of the spirit. On the other hand, the civilizations arising from other nations are oriented to earthly conditions and constraints. Unfortunately, these lead to double standards of morality and life, which create a gulf in understanding.

Israel is the eternal witness to the supremacy of the spiritual over the natural order. Israel's history is the history of the spirit; not of the natural, physical, social, or economic laws which govern the destiny of other nations. Israel's grandeur and Israel's decadence reflect the highs and lows in its moral and spiritual strength.

The Torah of Israel brings all human energies into play in order to triumph over nature and society through the power of the spirit. This power is capable of sanctifying all life. It strives to bring harmony into all factors of existence, and thereby to achieve the Kingdom of G-d on earth. This harmony is ennobled through the sacrifices made by each of the many elements of creation in order to unite with the others. It is sacrifice that gives this way of life its stamp of holiness and morality.

Every individual aspires to this ideal, it represents his primary purpose in life. The human soul desires to rise above material limitations and enjoy purely spiritual and moral satisfactions. The ultimate goal of the principle of harmony is to bring all beings to the accord with nature that originally existed in the garden of paradise.

Can Israel's philosophy ever be reconciled with that of other nations? The ideal of unity and harmony which comes from the belief in one G-d could never come to terms with the practices of double standards and compromises that are characteristic of the civilizations of the world. There is no way that Israel could join with those civilizations on their terms. To merit heavenly blessing, the Jew is asked to serve G-d "בכל לבבך ובכל נפשך ובכל מאודך, with all your heart, and your soul, and with all your might."

The only solution for establishing true harmony between Israel and the other nations is to raise all of mankind to Israel's ideal. This cannot be done by force, but will happen by itself through historical necessity. Whether realizing it or not, since the dawn of time, humanity has been committed to this unification. Swept along by an irresistible force, it has cast off the different forms of paganism and idol worshipping. It is progressively surmounting the religious systems that place intermediaries between the human soul and G-d. It is gradually triumphing over regimes that divide society into master and slave. Instinctively, it is moving towards the union of all men and all peoples in an era of justice and peace, an era crowned by the Kingdom of G-d.

Thus, the paths of Israel and the other nations are gradually coming together. The day will surely come when these paths will join. This must happen because truth, which is the same for all nations, must necessarily triumph. The suspicion felt by the other nations towards Israel will be replaced by respect and recognition of Israel as the keeper of the flame of eternal truth over thousands of years. Then hearts will open wide and Israel will share its spiritual heritage with all the nations and will offer them the universal framework for building the Kingdom of G-d.

In the final analysis, it is the reconciliation between Israel and the other nations that will bring about the restoration of universal harmony. For the achievement of Israel's ideal will result in the merging of all spheres of life—physical, ethical, spiritual, social, economic, and political—into a grand and powerful unity. That cosmic harmony will embrace all men and all of nature. Out of the brotherhood of all creatures will spring up the common worship of one G-d, the Father of all mankind. And so the ancient prophecy of Zechariah (14:19) will be fulfilled, "והיה ה' למלך על כל הארץ ביום ההוא יהיה ה' אחד ושמו אחד, The L-rd will be King over all the earth, on that day the L-rd will be One, and His Name will be One".

BIOGRAPHY OF
Rabbi Elie Munk ז״ל

by Rabbi Nosson Sherman

Rabbi Elie Munk was born in Paris on 21 Elul 5660 (1900). His father, R' Shmuel was an exemplar of Hirschian *Torah im Derech Eretz*; a Torah scholar and businessman who would not waver one iota in his loyalty to Torah and *mitzvos*, in his home, community, or business life. When he was only 11, Elie lost his mother. Because R' Shmuel's business often required him to be away from home for extended periods of time, he moved to Berlin, where he had brothers who could help him care for the children.

So it was that Elie's youth brought him in contact with three outstanding leaders in Berlin who had a profound influence on his life. The first was his uncle, Rabbi Ezriel Munk, rabbi of Berlin and a heroic battler for *shechitah*. The other two were leaders of the famed Hildesheimer Rabbinical Seminary where he studied: Rabbi David Zvi Hoffman, the famed *posek* who succeeded in discrediting the so-called "Higher Bible Criticism"; and Rabbi Avrohom Eliyohu Kaplan, the Lithuanian Talmudic genius, whose sudden death devastated the Berlin Torah community.

Such influences gave Rabbi Munk the combination of breadth and depth, and the searching philosophical approach that characterized him all his life. During his early 20's, he became attracted to the study of Kabbalah. In addition to a thorough knowledge of Shas, Shulchan Aruch, and Tanach, Rabbi Munk attained a mastery of the *Zohar* and the classics of Kabbalah. He used to say that his primary "teacher" in this field was R' Moshe Cordovero (בעל שיעור קומה, והפרדס ...).

Rabbi Munk's extensive writings flowed naturally from his career as a rabbi; for to him a spiritual leader had to be a teacher, personal guide, kashrus supervisor, founder of yeshivos, benefactor of refugees, and anything else the community might require. He excelled in his performance of אוהב שלום ורודף שלום, by stressing the search of peace in the community, respect among its members, and positive cooperation between each other. Among his perceived responsibilities was the duty to deepen the kehillah's Jewish knowledge through the eloquence and erudition of his tongue and pen. That is why he wrote in German and French rather than classical Hebrew; he wrote for the people, not libraries, so he wrote in the language of the people.

His first book, in German, was the classic *World of Prayer*. It has been translated into Hebrew, French, and English and is regarded by scholar and layman alike as one of the finest seforim of its kind. It is a magnificent commentary on the Siddur, that combines p'shat, halachah, and kabbalah. Most amazing is that he wrote it as the young *rabbiner* of Ansbach when he was only 28 years old! Only a year later, the leading *gaon* of the generation, Rabbi Chaim Ozer Grodzensky remarked to Rabbi Shimon Schwab, "all the rabbis of the Munk family are *tzaddikim*."

His other major work was written in French, when he was rabbi of Paris, where he came in 1937. *La Voix de Thora*, now being translated into English as "The Call of the Torah," demonstrates his mastery of the classical commentators such as *Ramban* and R' *Bachya* as well as Kabbalah and R' S. R. Hirsch. All are molded into a smooth-flowing, thoughtful and profound commentary that has played an important role in the recent upsurge of Torah life in France.

In Switzerland during the war years, he wrote *La Justice Sociale en Israel*, on social legislation in the Torah.

Rabbi Munk was married to the former Fanny Goldberger, whose father was president of the Orthodox community of Nurenberg. He said about his late beloved wife, "She was the perfect, invincible, happy optimist. Remember that without optimism, life loses its charm." Together they raised two sons and five daughters in a home that was always a busy center of community activity, a home of guests, and a haven to the perplexed, yet never failed to be a warm, closely knit, happy center of family life. Though the Munks were always serious, dedicated people, their family was suffused with humor and cheerfulness. When Rabbi Munk said that throughout his life, even in the bitter times of danger and flight from the Nazis, he never felt sadness or lost his joy in living, this seemingly astounding remark did not surprise those who knew him best. Indeed it was no exaggeration that people called him a living *Mesilas Yeshorim*. During his last years when he suffered from increasing infirmity and physical helplessness, a visitor once remarked that he was being given יסורין של אהבה, suffering as a sign of Heavenly love, he laughingly replied that he had never experienced suffering in his life.

This slim volume, *Ascent to Harmony*, was his final work, and, to his mind, in many ways his most important. It expresses his own philosophy of life: that is, one must marshal his every experience and thought, his knowledge, ability, and talent into a harmonious full life dedicated to the service of G-d. This book was the last manuscript he worked on; in a sense, it was his last will and testament, his personal statement as a Jew and talmid chacham. His entire life was a quest to embrace all areas of learning, all experiences permitted and regulated by the Torah, and all traits of his personality into a harmonious תפארת, the splendor of total harmony.